Wildlife
Intarsia

by Judy Gale Roberts and Jerry Booher

Fox
Chapel Publishing

1970 Broad Street • East Petersburg, PA 17520
www.FoxChapelPublishing.com

Wildlife Intarsia is an original work, first published in 2005 by Fox Chapel Publishing Company, Inc. The patterns contained herein are copyrighted by the authors. Readers may make eight copies of these patterns for personal use. The patterns themselves, however, are not to be duplicated for resale or distribution under any circumstances. Any such copying is a violation of copyright law.

ISBN 978–1–56523–282–2

Publisher's Cataloging-in-Publication Data

Roberts, Judy Gale.
    Wildlife intarsia / by Judy Gale Roberts and Jerry Booher. --
    East Petersburg, PA : Fox Chapel Publishing, c2005.

        p. ; cm.

        ISBN 978-1-56523-282-2

        1. Marquetry. 2. Wildlife wood-carving--Patterns. 3.
        Woodcarving—Patterns. I. Booher, Jerry. II. Title.

TT192 .R66 2005
745.51/2--dc22   0509

To learn more about the other great books
from Fox Chapel Publishing, or to find a
retailer near you, call toll-free 800-457-9112
or visit us at **www.FoxChapelPublishing.com**.

Note to Authors: We are always looking for talented authors
to write new books in our area of woodworking, design, and related
crafts. Please send a brief letter describing your idea to Peg Couch,
Acquisition Editor, 1970 Broad Street, East Petersburg, PA 17520.

Printed in China
10 9 8 7 6 5 4 3 2

Because scrolling wood and other materials inherently includes the risk of injury and damage, this book cannot guarantee that creating the projects in this book is safe for everyone. For this reason, this book is sold without warranties or guarantees of any kind, expressed or implied, and the publisher and the authors disclaim any liability for any injuries, losses, or damages caused in any way by the content of this book or the reader's use of the tools needed to complete the projects presented here. The publisher and the authors urge all scrollers to thoroughly review each project and to understand the use of all tools before beginning any project.

Contents

The artist largely responsible for the rebirth of intarsia, Judy Gale Roberts began creating intarsia with her father, Pat Dudley Roberts, around 1974. The two designed custom wood murals, among other artwork, for some of their clients.

In 1984, Jerry Booher came onboard, and Judy began to design and create one-of-a-kind pieces on a smaller scale for private collections. Jerry, a tool and die maker before switching careers, studied and refined the process that Judy and her father used and became an expert on the scroll saw. It was also in 1984 that Jerry sent pictures to the National Woodcarvers Association asking if they knew of a name for this technique of woodworking. The Association wrote back with the name, "intarsia," stating that the only place they had seen it was in Italy.

Throughout the 1980s, Judy and Jerry attended juried shows and won a number of ribbons for their intarsia work. In the process of competing in shows, the two began to educate and expose the world to the art form called intarsia.

In 1997, Judy was the first woman and one of the first 10 people to be inducted into *Wood* magazine's Woodworking Hall of Fame. Her work has been featured in *Wood* magazine, *Scroll Saw Workshop*, and Patrick Spielman's *The Art of the Scroll Saw*.

At present, Judy and Jerry teach almost 100 students each year in beginning, inter-mediate, advanced intarsia techniques, and their pattern business has grown from its initial three patterns to 300 patterns.

Getting Started

This intarsia pattern book of American wildlife is an accumulative representation of over two decades of creating intarsia works of art. This book combines both Jerry Booher's scroll sawing/precision skills and my, Judy Gale Roberts', designs, wood selection, and shaping skills. Although this is a pattern book, we've included some basic instructions to get you started and how-to instructions for the first three demonstrations. We felt it was important to include these instructions for those of you who are just beginning to learn about intarsia and for those of you who want to improve upon your skills.

If you have never done intarsia before, the basic process involves studying your project, choosing tools and materials, cutting the pieces, shaping the pieces through sanding, and assembling and finishing the project. We'll cover the general ideas here and get into more detail for the first three demonstrations.

Each of the projects in this book was designed with a scroll saw in mind; however, the patterns can be modified to use a band saw. On each pattern, you will notice a legend showing grain direction, tones of wood colors, and areas to be raised with ¼" shims. All of these projects were cut from ¾"-thick wood.

Pattern preparation and layout

Before you start working on any project, study the pattern. This is a good habit to learn; the ability to anticipate problems will make your work more enjoyable.

First, measure the sections to determine how much wood you'll need or if the sections will fit the wood that you have. Let's use the Bald Eagle pattern as an example (see **Photo 1.1**). In the Bald Eagle, measure the width of the two *W* neck parts to make sure you have a piece of white wood that is wide enough to lay out these two sections as one piece. It measures 8" across; therefore, if you do not have an 8"-wide piece of white wood, you will cut out these pattern sections individually. Also note where the pattern's focus is and think about what wood you want to use for the different sections.

Next, we'll determine which parts may be a little tougher to saw out. It is easier to see any difficulties as you are looking at the whole pattern rather than at the individual pattern pieces. Perhaps we'll cut out the easier parts first; then, when we feel comfortable at the saw, we'll cut out the more challenging parts.

Transferring the Pattern

There are two ways to transfer the pattern to the wood. One is to use carbon or graphite paper, and the other is to use repositionable adhesive to adhere copies of the pattern to the wood.

Using Carbon Paper

If you choose this method, you will only need one copy of the pattern. Start by placing the pattern over the wood, following the grain direction. When you are happy with the placement, hold the pattern in place with a couple of pushpins on one edge. Then, slide the carbon paper under the pattern and place a couple more pins to keep the pattern from shifting. Put the pushpins on the edges of the wood, so that you don't end up with holes on the surfaces' good parts. Sometimes the pin hole doesn't show up until you put the finish on.

If we are transferring the parts on white wood, we'll transfer all of the *W* parts; then, we'll move on to the *M* (medium shade) wood, and so on until all of the parts have been transferred to the different shades of wood.

Using Adhesive

The other method of transferring the pattern requires making multiple copies of the pattern, cutting the sections out, and gluing them to the wood. Cutting the paper pattern into sections makes the layout process much easier. You can really move the pattern pieces around to get the best grain for each part. Almost all of the projects will need at least six copies based on the number of shades used and the grain direction.

Photo 1.1. Study the pattern before you begin a project, looking for potential problems in laying out the pattern on the wood and in cutting the pattern pieces.

Copying the pattern. Make all copies of the pattern at the same time because not all copiers are created the same. Copies from one machine may stretch the pattern one way or another. Distortions can even show up if you use the same copier from one day to the next. We like to make a couple of extra copies—one for the "master copy" and an extra one, just in case.

Again using the Bald Eagle pattern as an example, notice that you will need six copies of the pattern—two copies for the white wood (because the grain direction is not the same), one copy for the light-colored parts, one for the medium parts, one for the dark parts, and one for your master copy. If the wood is not wide enough for any sections of the white shades, you can cut each *W* piece out individually. You may need to add extra pattern copies for the parts you will cut individually. Most of the time, we like to keep sections of the pattern that have the same color and grain direction together to be cut out as a unit, and then we part the individual sections on the saw.

Labeling your master copy. We like to number each part on the master because it makes assembling the project easier when you are checking for fit. Then, cut the different sections out of the copies, leaving about a ¼" border around the line work. By leaving the border, you end up cutting into the adjoining parts. Those parts will need to be cut from another copy of the pattern. Transfer the numbers from the master onto the pattern parts (see **Photo 1.2**). **Tip:** Numbering the pattern before making photocopies will save you time.

After the pattern is separated into general areas, mark those areas that are outside edges. We use a series of arrows to mark these sections. You can relax as you cut these outside edges because nothing has to fit next to them. After the pattern is cut up, we put the pieces in piles by shade. All of the pieces labeled *W* go in one pile, all of the *LT* ones go in another, and so on for each shade used.

Photo 1.2. Cut out the different sections, leaving a ¼" border around the line work. Transfer the numbers from the master copy to the parts, and mark the outside edges, as we have done with arrows.

Gluing the pattern to the wood. First, get your wood as dust free as possible. We use a temporary adhesive that allows us to unstick and restick the pattern pieces, such as a repositionable glue stick or a repositionable spray adhesive. The trick to using the glue stick, a water-based product, is to put the glue on the paper and let it dry for about 20 to 30 seconds before sticking the paper to the wood. The waiting time allows the glue to dry a little and then to stick better. It is also a good idea to burnish the pattern down for extra "staying power." We use the cap of the glue stick, pressing hard and rubbing it over the surface of the pattern. Arts and crafts stores also sell a plastic burnisher, which looks like a thick putty knife with rounded edges.

When using spray adhesive, you need to wait 20 to 30 seconds to let the glue set and to make it easier to peel the pattern pieces off the parts after they have been cut out. If you apply the spray adhesive while it is too wet, it makes a more permanent bond. With either type of glue, be sure to put enough glue evenly on the pattern. There is nothing more frustrating than a pattern that starts flapping loose while you are cutting a critical area. Also, trim any excess paper flush with the edge of the board; otherwise, it will start to peel back.

Choosing Your Wood

Use whatever wood you have on hand for these projects, especially if you are just starting out. It will take some time to build up an inventory of various shades of wood. Going through the motions will give you more experience, so do not let "I don't have the right kind of wood" stop you from gaining more knowledge through practice. Whatever wood you do choose, make sure that your lumber is dry. A moisture meter is a good investment.

Wood Size and Thickness

Most lumber comes somewhat smooth on three sides: the face side and both edges. We run the rough side through a planer, taking off just enough so the board lies flat. Clean up both sides if needed; however, try to keep the wood as thick as possible.

The larger the project, the more flat it will look—unless you use thicker wood. For a small project that would fit on an 8½" by 11" pattern, ½"-thick wood will make the project look dimensional. The same ½"-thick material on a 17" by 23" project will make it look flat, regardless of how much sanding you do. We use ¾"-thick wood on projects within the 17" by 23" range. On projects 20" by 30" or larger, use 1"- to 1½"-thick material.

Color and Grain

We use western red cedar for 98 percent of our projects because we like its array of colors and grain patterns; however, any type of wood can be used. The color and grain patterns are more important than the type of wood (see **Photo 1.3**). For our white wood, we often use aspen. It keeps its nice, warm-white color even after the finish has been applied.

If you go to a lumberyard for western red cedar, be sure to ask for it by its entire name. It is often confused with eastern cedar or aromatic red cedar, which are used in closets and similar applications. Aromatic red cedar can be used for intarsia, but it does not have the color variety that western red cedar has. Red cedar can work for areas that would look great in red, like a cardinal, but we noticed that red cedar tends to darken quickly to brown.

If you have access to unusual wood, it can also work well with intarsia projects. Try incorporating natural parts of a log (see **Photo 1.4**) or using spalted wood (see **Photos 1.5** and **1.6**). Spalting is created when the wood is rotting.

You may also want to look for boards that have knots. Many times wood grain is very unusual around knots and can be used to accentuate certain parts of an intarsia project. However, if every piece of wood on the project has a strong, unusual grain pattern, it can take away from the overall effect of the finished piece (see **Photo 1.7**).

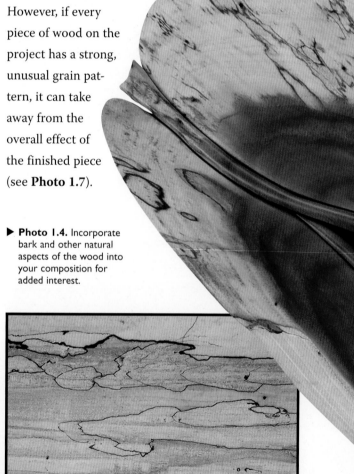

▶ **Photo 1.4.** Incorporate bark and other natural aspects of the wood into your composition for added interest.

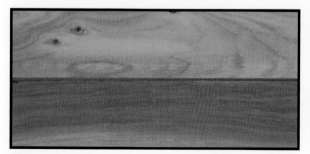

Photo 1.3. Look for a variety of grain patterns. Boards with varied color within them work great for intarsia.

Photo 1.5. Spalted wood gives Intarsia projects a unique look.

Wood Choice for Pattern Layout

Decide what the main focus of the pattern will be, and look for an unusual grain pattern in a piece of wood to make these areas more interesting and stand out more. My theory for laying the pattern parts on the wood is as follows: Put what would be the main pattern parts on the wood first, giving them top priority; then place the other parts around those. For example, if we were laying out a horse head, we would put the major parts of the horse's head in the best grain placement possible; then, we would fill in with the secondary parts of the same color, like the ears.

If you plan to use woodburned or carved textures on any parts, the grain configuration isn't as important. Save your unusual grain patterns for areas that will need the extra emphasis.

Always check both sides of the board when you lay out your pieces. Sometimes a knot may angle into one of the project's parts. Also, if you are using a board's natural highlight, be sure to check both sides of the wood and the edge grain, if possible, to see how deep the lighter color goes.

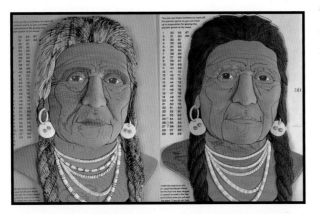

▲ **Photo 1.6.** The Indian on the left was made using spalted wood. He looks much older than the Indian on the right, which has walnut for the hair. (Finish has not yet been applied to either of these Indians.)

▲ **Photo 1.7.** Duck #1 incorporates too much grain activity. Duck #2 is more pleasing to the eye, and the heavy grain on the wing stands out beautifully.

Scroll sawing

Before you begin scrolling, make sure that the saw blade is square to the table. This can be done with a small square (see **Photo 1.8**). You'll also want to check all of the parts to be cut for the burr on the bottom side, and remove it if it is present. The burr will make your pieces sit unevenly on the saw and throw off an otherwise perfectly square cut.

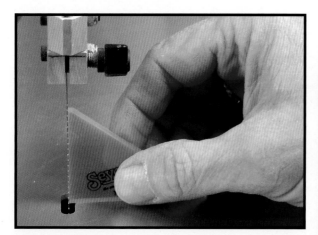

Photo 1.8. Check to make sure that the table is square to the blade.

Check the pattern to see if there are any blade entry holes needed. On the Bald Eagle project, for example, you will need to drill blade entry holes if you plan to inlay the nostril and the pupil in the center of the eye. If you choose not to inlay these parts, you can wood-burn these areas after the parts have been shaped.

Order of Cutting

Cut out all of the color sections first, and then slice up the individual parts. When you are sawing the color sections, start sawing on the outside areas of the project first. The outside edges don't have to fit next to other parts, so you don't have to worry if you drift off the line. As we are sawing the outside lines, we try to get the feel of the blade and the material. On the parts that have to fit next to other parts, use caution, especially when the parts that will fit together are dif-

ferent colors. When different color parts are involved, the sawing must be more accurate than when all of the parts are the same color and grain direction.

If you are new to sawing, put the middle of the blade on the middle of the line, removing all of the layout line (see **Photo 1.9**). If you are a seasoned pro, you can saw to the outside of the layout line and leave about half of the line.

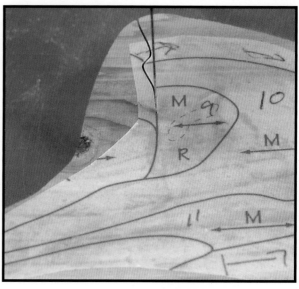

Photo 1.9. Put your blade in the center of the line.

Take into account that different woods may need different blades (see the A Word About Scroll Saw Blades section on page 8 for more information). For instance, we use a different saw blade for aspen than we do for western red cedar. Cut all of the parts that use a particular blade at the same time, so that you don't have to keep switching between blades.

After all of the parts have been cut, turn each part over to the backside and remove any burr or tear out. Transfer the number of the piece from the pattern to the back. If you do not put the number on the back, at least put an *X*. This will help you to identify which side is the bottom of the part when you begin sanding.

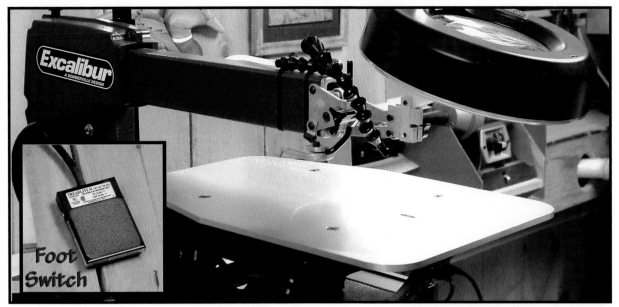

Photo 1.10. A foot switch and a magnifier with a light are great assets for scroll sawing.

Useful Accessories

There are two additional pieces of equipment that we use along with the saw. One is a foot switch and the other is a magnifier/light. The foot switch is a very important addition to a scroll saw. It allows you to have both hands on the work piece before starting the saw, and it will also allow you to turn off the saw with both hands still holding the work piece. A foot switch is especially handy when you are in a cut and want to get a better, or different, grip on the work piece. Simply stop the saw to get a better grip and then start it up again. The foot switch is a must-have item for safety, convenience, and accuracy (see **Photo 1.10**).

The magnifier/light is another very important addition. Magnifiers run the gamut as far as pricing goes. We use a magnifier/light that has a ground glass lens of the same quality used in eyeglasses. Cheaper magnifier/lights are available, but you get what you pay for. You can expect to pay around $250 for a good magnifier/light.

Hand Tools

We also use a few hand tools when we are sawing. One tool is a small square, which we use to check the parts to see if the cut is square to the bottom. The next tool is a sander of some kind to remove the burr,

or tear out, on the bottom side of the piece being sawed (see **Photo 1.11**). Last but not least, we use a wooden craft stick to hold the pattern down should it start to come off as we are sawing.

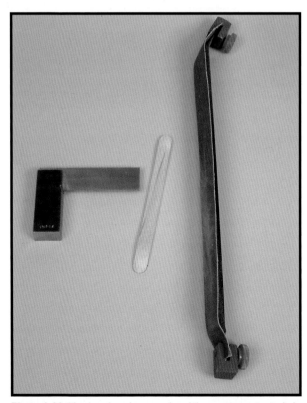

Photo 1.11. Hand tools to have nearby while you are sawing include a square (check often to make sure you are cutting square), a wooden craft stick (to help hold down a loose pattern while sawing), and a flat Detail Sander (to remove the burr on the backside of the wood).

A word about scroll saw blades

The question we are asked most often is, "What scroll saw blades do you use?" The choice of which blade to use is really a matter of personal preference. We'll list the blades we use in our shop, but be sure to experiment to find which blades best fit your working style.

Plain-end versus Pin-end

The first thing you'll want to note is whether you need pin- or plain-end blades (see **Photo 1.12**). The type of saw you have will determine the type of blade that you need. Saws that accept pin-end blades have a slot where the pin sits. Saws that accept plain-end blades have clamps that grasp the ends of the blade. Some saws will accept both types of blades.

Pin-end blades are usually used for entry-level saws. While pin-end blades can be easier to align because

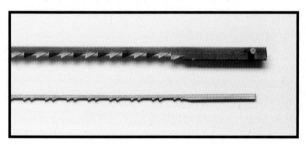

Photo 1.12. The pin of a pin-end blade allows the blade to be fastened to the scroll saw. Pin-end blades are typically much larger than plain-end blades.

the pin sits in a slot, they come in limited tooth configurations and in limited sizes. Also, pin-end blades must be large in order for the pin to fit in the blade. The larger blade size will limit the blade's turning ability and its ability to make inside cuts due to the large hole that must be drilled to accommodate the pin.

Plain-end blades come in a variety of tooth configurations and sizes. These blades are more popular and come in smaller sizes than pin-end blades, making detailed work easier (see Photo 1.12). Because these blades clamp in without the pin as a guide, it is especially important to check that the blade is square to the table.

Tooth Configuration

Because we work with plain-end blades, we'll use them as examples for tooth configuration. There are a number of different types. Some of the most common are regular tooth blades, skip tooth blades (where every other tooth is eliminated, giving more chip clearance), and reverse skip tooth blades (where five to seven teeth at the bottom of the blade reverse direction). There is even a round blade that will cut in all different directions.

Because there are so many choices, it is fairly difficult to pick a blade that will work on all materials. Experimentation may be the best way to decide what blades work best for you. In most cases, we use reverse skip tooth blades. Reverse tooth blades usually give a cleaner finish on the bottom side of the part.

When a reverse skip tooth blade is mounted in the saw, the teeth cut on the upstroke as well as on the downstroke. The five to seven reverse teeth should be on the lower bottom end. You'll want to be sure that the blade is mounted properly because it will saw even if it is upside down. A tale-tell sign that the blade is upside down is that it tears the edge of the pattern as you are sawing. Reverse tooth blades may also have a tendency to "lift" the workpiece up on the upstroke.

Material	Thickness	Blade Size	Tooth Configuration
Aspen	under ¾"	#5 Platinum	Reverse skip tooth
Aspen	over ¾"	#7 Platinum	Reverse skip tooth
Western Red Cedar	under ¾"	#5 Gold	Reverse skip tooth
Western Red Cedar	over ¾"	#5 or #7 Platinum	Reverse skip tooth
Walnut	under ¾"	#5 Gold or Platinum	Reverse skip tooth
Walnut	over ¾"	#7 Gold or Platinum	Reverse skip tooth

Blade Sizes

The blade size you choose is based on the thickness of the material that you're using and on the size of kerf that you want. Normally, we use a #5 blade to saw wood that is ¾" thick or less. For thicker material, we use a #7 blade (see **Photo 1.13**). To slice up parts, we use a #2 or smaller, depending on the material we are cutting. We switch to a smaller blade for the individual parts because the smaller blade gives a smaller kerf and, therefore, a better fit.

You'll also want to take into account the type of wood that you're cutting. Because we use aspen for our white wood, we will use a different saw blade than we use for the western red cedar. For example, we use an On-Line #7 Platinum blade for aspen and an On-Line #5 Gold blade for western red cedar. The Platinum blade is a more aggressive saw blade that works best for aspen because aspen wears out blades faster than western red cedar. Both the Gold and Platinum blades are reverse skip tooth blades.

As you can see from this section, choosing a blade can be a complex and time-consuming task. The best advice we can give you is to get a big fistful of blades and a stack of lumber and start cutting. Experience will help you decide.

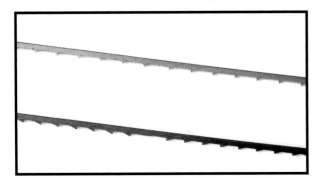

Photo 1.13. Plain-end blades are available in a variety of sizes. Reverse tooth plain-end blades, shown here, usually give a cleaner finish on the bottom side of the part.

Checking for fit

Once you have finished cutting and before you remove the pattern, look over the project to see if everything is fitting properly (see **Photo 1.14**). Any line work that

Photo 1.14. Check to see that everything fits before removing the paper.

shows on the pattern may reveal a problem with the fit. If there is line work evident and there is a fit problem, mark that part and trim it with the saw. We use a new, sharp blade in the scroll saw to trim any parts. Practice shaving the edges of outside edge parts, or lay out some areas with which to practice, before you trim the project pieces. If there are no lines showing at all and the parts don't fit, you may need to re-cut some parts.

You do not want to sand between parts to make them fit, especially before anything is shaped, because you can end up with parts that are "out of square." While they may fit on the top, the space between the parts may grow when you start sanding and lowering pieces. This is why we use the scroll saw and a new blade, rather than sanding, to trim the project pieces. Trimming helps to ensure that the parts will remain square.

Sanding and shaping

Before you begin sanding and shaping, take a minute to study the project again. We like to get a general idea of how we will tackle the project. It is best to rough-in the entire project, and then go back and add the detail as needed. Start by lowering background parts, or the parts that would be the farthest from the viewer. To determine which parts are farthest from the viewer, note which parts are behind other parts. For instance, on an animal that is facing sideways, one of the ears would be behind the head. Use the photos of the finished pieces to guide you.

Using Shims

At this point, we check to see if we need to make any shims to raise some parts. If we want to sand some sections together, we will make what we call "sanding shims." Sanding shims are simply pieces of ¼" luan plywood that temporarily hold pieces together as you are sanding. These shims allow you to sand multiple pieces as though they are one piece of wood. In many cases, making sanding shims saves time, and there is less handling of each part. We use sanding shims on almost all of the projects to get a consistent contour and flow to the piece. Even though the color or the wood changes in a project, it doesn't mean that the contour should change between the colors of the wood.

On the patterns, we have indicated areas where we used a ¼" piece of plywood to raise parts. Only raise interior parts; a shim exposed on the outside edge of a project just doesn't look very nice. If you must raise an outside part, use the same color wood and laminate the two parts together to get the desired thickness. The easiest method is to use thick wood; then, you will not need any raising shims.

For the sanding process, we like to have at least two pieces of double-sided tape to hold each part down to the shim. We use the least expensive double-sided tape we can find because it doesn't have too strong of a bond. Remember, you don't want the bond to be permanent for the sanding process. We will only be using the sanding shims temporarily, and we will glue the raising shims in place once the shaping is complete.

Also, it is best not to leave the sections taped up overnight. It seems that the longer the double-sided tape sits, the harder it is to take the sections apart. We prefer to put the double-sided tape on the backsides of the parts when we can, as opposed to putting it on the sanding shim, because it is easier to see where the

tape needs to go. If you put double-sided tape on the shim first, you will need to cover most of the surface to make sure all of the parts will have enough tape on them. However, if you are using multiple raising shims, it is easier to put double-sided tape on the raising shims and then place each part onto the raising shim. If, as you're sanding, any parts start to come off, stop and take the time to retape them.

Working at the Sander

When you are sanding your project, keep all of the parts nearby. We assemble the parts on the pattern and place the project on a cart with wheels that we put right next to the sander (see **Photo 1.15**). With the project close to the sander, you can easily put the part back in place to see if you want to remove more or less material. Remember, once you remove wood, you can't put it back. If you are ever uncertain when you are sanding a part, put it back in place and even mark on the surface where you want to sand. If we are not familiar with the subject matter, we will find as many pictures as possible to aid in shaping.

Photo 1.15. I keep my project on a wheeled cart right next to me as I sand. If I have any doubts about where to sand, I can easily look at the project and refresh my memory.

It is best to use a soft, flexible sander and press the parts you are sanding firmly against the drum. The softness of the sander makes it easier to get flowing, smooth contours. Use an air-filled drum or a flexible foam-type sander for best results. A belt sander or a disc sander will work also. We have two drums: one large one (9" diameter) with a 100-grit sleeve and one small one (2½" diameter) with a 180-grit sleeve (see Photo 1.15 and **Photo 1.16**).

Photo 1.16. A soft sander like the Flex Drum Sander DS-1 will make it easier to get the soft contours.

The shaping process is really a matter of marking the areas to sand and then sanding according to your marks. Guard against the cycle of sanding one part down too much, then sanding too much off an adjoining part, then sanding the first part down some more, and so on. This cycle can lead to a project in need of plastic surgery. It is important to learn to watch your pencil lines and to stay above them, to put the part in place to check your progress, and to slowly sand off a little at a time.

Adding texture

We often use a tool called the Wonder Wheel to add texture to intarsia projects (or any woodworking project). It works best on softer woods; however, it will work on hard woods too. When used with a soft wood like western red cedar, it will carve and burnish the wood in one stroke. It has a tendency to burn more than carve on the harder woods, and the harder woods will wear out the wheel much faster. The wheel looks as if it is as hard as a stone, but it has some give

to it. If you don't have a Wonder Wheel, you can use a V-shaped carving tool to gouge out the texture.

We find it easier to keep the wheel stationary as we move the piece of wood to get the texture we want. Many times the pieces we're texturing are small, and it is hard to hold onto the part in one hand, use a rotary power tool in the other hand, and then try to put texture on the part. If you are using a hand tool, you may need to clamp the part down to put texture on it.

Dressing the Wheel

The wheel is 6" in diameter and ½" wide. The ½"-wide surface is flat when it arrives from the factory (see **Photo 1.17**). It needs to run at least 3450 rpm; 4000 rpm is the maximum speed. It is important to follow the rotation arrows on the wheel. We use a piece of coarse sanding cloth or paper (from 40 grit to 60 grit) stapled to a flat piece of wood to dress the wheel (see **Photo 1.18**). Using firm pressure, you will sand the

Photo 1.17. The Wonder Wheel is flat on the edge when it comes from the factory. For most texturing, it is better to make the flat edge into a V shape.

Photo 1.18. To make the flat edge into a V shape, we staple a piece of coarse sandpaper to a flat piece of wood. Sand a 45-degree angle on both sides.

sides to a point or a V shape. Keep moving the sandpaper; it will get hot if you stay in one spot for too long. Once you have the V shape, it will not take as long to re-sharpen it. The V shape seems to work for most textures we have applied.

Once you have a sharp corner and begin using it to apply texture, it will wear and lose its edge, so it will need to be re-sharpened from time to time. If the wheel dances around or is hard to control, these signs may indicate that it needs to be re-sharpened.

Photo 1.19. The wheel works great for eyes made from dowels or pieces of wood. Going over the surface of the wood will burnish and darken the wood.

Using the Wheel

The wheel will burn and polish dowels used for eyes or any piece of wood used for the eye. To get the best results, go with the grain as much as possible (see **Photo 1.19**). When you're using the wheel for various textures—for example, a bear's rougher coat—make a series of short, deep strokes, keeping the wheel sharp to make chisel-like grooves. On a project with a soft coat, like a Collie or a horse's mane, let the wheel get a little more rounded and make long, flowing strokes.

The amount of pressure applied is also important. It doesn't take a lot of pressure to make a texture that will show up. If you are putting texture on a dog, for example, you may want to apply very little pressure around the eye and nose area to give the impression of a smoother coat. As you get to the sides of the face, you can add more pressure, which will make it look like a coarser, thicker coat.

Texture is a nice contrast to all of the smooth pieces of wood. When we add texture, we basically cover the entire surface with a series of grooves. If you go with the grain, it will make a smoother groove. The Wonder Wheel works well for creating detail for a rope, and, in this case, it will save time. The individual rope segments can be carved with the wheel rather than cut individually (see **Photo 1.20**).

Using a Woodburner

The woodburner can be hard to control for the novice at woodburning. Inlaying a part is often an easier option. The larger the surface area to be burned, the harder it is to burn evenly. A large, round area like the pupil can be especially challenging to burn evenly. Burning a nostril is a much easier task; we would use the woodburner over inlaying for a part that small.

We find it best to use a knifelike burning tip to do any detail. The sharp edge cuts through the grain, and the side works great for shading. If you burn a pupil, make the outer curved line cut through the grain like a knife. Then, place the burning tip on its side to shade the rest of the pupil. It's a good idea to draw lots of whatever part you're burning on some scrap wood and practice before burning the actual part.

Photo 1.20. You can use the wheel to make a ropelike texture. Carving these sections rather than cutting each rope section individually can save time. Note how it carves and darkens each line.

Photo 1.21. Hand sand each part, looking for any bumps or scratches. Sand the edges also, knocking off the sharp corners of all parts.

Hand sand each part

Once you have finished texturing, hand sand each part. Hold the parts up to the light to see if there are any humps, bumps, or scratches. When you hold the parts up to the light, it will help you to spot areas that need more work. It is better to do this now rather than when the finished piece is hanging on your wall and all you see are the imperfections. Hand sand the edges, barely knocking off the sharp corners on all parts (see **Photo 1.21**). Erase any pencil lines that may be showing, and check again for any deep scratches.

Applying the finish

Before you apply the finish, be sure to read and follow the manufacturers' recommendations and cautions for applying their finishes. There are many finishes on the market today as well as many techniques for applying them. We will share our finishing method here, but you can choose the finishing method that you prefer.

We use a polyurethane wiping gel, which is applied to each part before the project is glued to the backing. Notice how the gel brings out the richness of the wood (see **Photo 1.22**). We begin by removing any dust with an air compressor. The entire part is dusted, including the edges and back.

Tools for Finishing

We need a few aids for applying and removing the gel. For applying the gel, we use a 1" disposable foam brush, some paper towels, a terry cloth towel, and a piece of scrap ¼" plywood to use as a paddle to remove the gel from the can (see **Photo 1.23**).

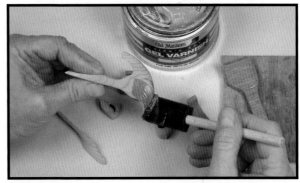

Photo 1.22. Notice how rich the color of the wood is with a coat of gel.

Photo 1.23. A disposable foam brush, paper towels, a terry cloth for wiping textured parts, and a paddle for scooping are needed to finish the pieces.

Applying the Gel

After opening the can, we turn the lid over and use the paddle to remove some gel. We place the gel on the underside of the lid and then place the lid, upside down, back on the can. If you work out of an open can, it's likely that a "skin" will form over the gel. Placing the lid on the can cuts off any airflow that could dry the gel. If a skin does develop, it can be removed, providing that it is not too thick.

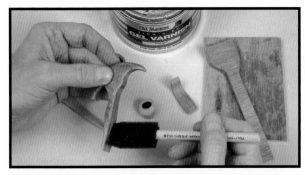

Photo 1.24. The gel is forgiving. Work with the top on the can to keep the gel from drying out in the can.

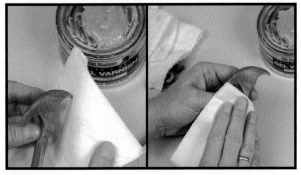

Photo 1.25. Use folded paper towels to wipe off the excess gel and to buff the pieces.

When applying the gel, be sure to use a liberal amount, especially on the first coat. Apply the gel to the sanded side of the part and to all of the edges. Do not coat the back of the part. Notice that my thumb is in contact with the coated side as I coat the edges (see **Photo 1.24**). The gel is very forgiving in this manner, and where my thumb made contact, I just apply a little more gel to the spot.

Removing the Gel

Once the gel has been applied to a few parts, it is ready to wipe off in about one minute. We use paper towels (a full sheet, folded into fourths) to wipe the

gel off the parts. Use one towel to wipe off the excess and go around the edges; then, use a fresh towel to buff the part, making sure to buff with the grain (see **Photo 1.25**). Normally the first towel and the buffing towel can be used for four or five parts before the towels need to be changed. When it's time to change the towels, use a new towel for the buffing towel and use the old buffing towel to wipe off the excess gel. We will coat two or three pieces before we start to wipe off the parts. We wipe all of the parts and then start the process over again until all of the parts have been coated. If, by chance, a part has been left too long before wiping, the gel will become tacky. Just apply more gel to the part, wait a few seconds, and then start wiping.

Finishing White Woods

Often white woods, like white pine or basswood, have a tendency to yellow or turn tan after the first coat of gel is applied. To keep the white parts looking white, apply a coat of white gel as the first coat. White gel is the same gel with a white pigment added. The more coats of white used, the more opaque the wood will look. When we use the white gel, we use just one coat to keep the color looking natural. If you want to stain the white wood, add an oil color to the gel and apply that mix as the first coat. Be sure to do some tests on scrap pieces of wood first.

Cleaning Up

For cleaning our hands, we use a waterless hand cleaner first and then wash them with soap and water. The foam brush can be wrapped in plastic wrap or in a plastic bag and can be used again for up to three days.

Making a backing

After the gel has dried, we use ¼" luan plywood or masonite to make a backing. It's best to trace around the actual parts, rather than to use the pattern, because many times you'll sand the edges or alter the shape of the original pattern in one way or another. Coat a piece of paper lightly with spray adhesive and assemble the parts on it. This keeps the parts from sliding around while you trace the outline.

After you trace the outline and remove the parts, use more adhesive spray and stick the paper to ¼" luan plywood. When you saw the backing, stay to the inside of the line, about ⅟₃₂" to ⅟₁₆". This careful cutting will make the backing a little smaller than the project and will ensure that the backing does not hang out past the project after the pieces are glued down.

Finishing the Backing

After the backing is cut, stain the edge with a dark brown leather dye (see **Photo 1.26**). The dye is alcohol based and dries very quickly. If you are using masonite, there is no need to stain the backing. We sand the backside of the backing to remove any of the dye that may have run. Do not sand the front side of the backing (the gluing surface). To help seal the entire project, we spray clear acrylic on the backside and on the edges of the backing. Assemble the parts on the backing to check how the project fits.

Photo 1.26. We use a leather dye to stain the edge of the backing.

Gluing the parts to the backing

We use a combination of yellow wood glue and hot melt glue to attach the parts to the backing. The hot glue acts as a clamp until the yellow wood glue dries. If you plan on using a hot glue gun, you will need a gun that heats up to at least 350 degrees; otherwise, your parts will not lie flat against the backing. The hot glue will cool and harden before you have time to press the piece into place.

First choose a key piece as the first piece to glue down. This piece will "lock" the rest of the project in place. Use yellow wood glue and hot glue on the locking piece. The remainder of the pieces can be glued down with only yellow wood glue.

Installing the hanger

We use a mirror hanger to hang our intarsia projects. This method has proven to be strong and reliable, and it is also adjustable. Mirror hangers come in a variety of sizes and can be found at home improvement centers as well as many hardware stores. For the projects in this book, we used a small hanger (see **Photo 1.27**). You could also choose a saw-toothed hanger, but we have found that these hangers cause the project to hang crooked.

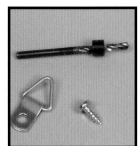

Photo 1.27. We use a mirror hanger instead of a saw tooth hanger because it is strong, reliable, and adjustable.

Regardless of the method you use to hang your finished project, you must first find out where the center of the project is. To do this, use your thumb and middle finger and pinch the project. Let it hang between your fingers, changing the location of your fingers until the correct balance point is found (see **Photo 1.28**). Mark the backing right at your fingertip, and drill the hole for the screw there. We always drill the hole slightly smaller than the screw we use to hold the mirror hanger, which is a #6 x ½" sheet metal screw.

Mark your drill for the depth to make sure that you don't drill all the way through the project. Make sure that the area you choose to drill is at least ⅝" thick. Keep in mind that the backing is ¼" thick, so you will only be drilling into the actual piece about ¼". After drilling the hole, install the mirror hanger. Don't tighten the screw too much; it only needs to be tight enough so that the hanger can swivel from right to left. This swing allows you to adjust the project so it will hang straight on the wall.

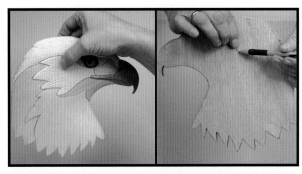

Photo 1.28. Hold the project with two fingers to find the balance point. Then, mark the back to show where to drill your hole.

Bald Eagle Demonstration

Tools
- Scroll saw (or band saw)
- Sander for contouring
- Drill
- Carving or X-Acto knife
- Woodburner (optional)

Wood
- White wood: aspen, white pine, poplar, holly, basswood, or any very light-colored wood; 8" wide by 24" long by 1" thick
- Light wood: western red cedar, oak, maple, or birch; 3" wide by 6" long by 1" thick
- Medium wood: western red cedar, butternut, cherry, mahogany, or pecan; 3" wide by 5" long by 1" thick
- Dark wood: western red cedar, walnut, ebony, or wenge; 2" wide by 2 ½" long by 1" thick
- ¼" luan plywood for the backing

Materials
- Repositionable spray adhesive
- Six copies of the Bald Eagle pattern
- Yellow wood glue
- Double-sided tape
- Hot melt glue and glue gun
- Polyurethane wiping gel or finish of choice
- Paper towels
- Lint-free terry cloth towel
- 1" disposable foam brush
- Brown leather dye
- Clear acrylic spray
- Mirror hanger or hanger of choice

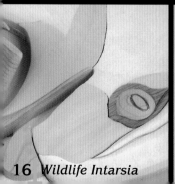

Enlarge pattern 110%

© Judy Gale Roberts and Jerry Booher

Make at least 6 copies of the Bald Eagle pattern.

Legend	
←——→	**Grain direction**
D	**Dark shade of wood**
M	**Medium shade of wood**
LT	**Light shade of wood**
W	**White pine, aspen, or any white wood**

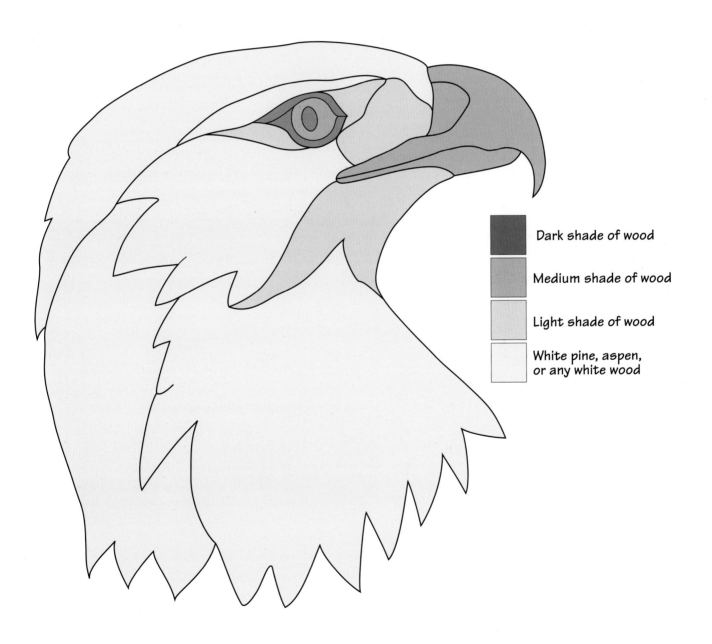

■ Dark shade of wood

■ Medium shade of wood

□ Light shade of wood

□ White pine, aspen, or any white wood

Photo 2.1. Map out the parts before actually cutting up the pattern.

Pattern preparation and layout

Step 1 Study the Bald Eagle pattern. It has only four colors of wood: *W* (white), *LT* (light), *M* (medium), and *D* (dark).

Step 2 Because the grain direction for the white wood does not go in the same direction for each part, you will need two copies for the white wood. Make all six of your photocopies at the same time: you'll need two copies for the white wood, one copy for the light-colored parts, one for the medium parts, one for the dark parts, and one for your master. If the wood is not wide enough for any sections, you can cut the piece individually. Make an extra copy if that is the case. **Photo 2.1** shows the mapping of the white pattern parts individually.

Step 3 Note where the main focus of the pattern will be. Then, look for an unusual grain pattern in a piece of wood to make these areas more interesting and stand out more. In this project, the focus is the Bald Eagle's eye. If you plan to use woodburned or carved textures on any parts, the grain configuration isn't as important.

TIP: The parts are placed on the wood. We found a darker shade of aspen for the *LT* area under the neck to help create a subtle shadow. This will help make the eagle look more dimensional than it is. We found a great piece of wood for the beak also.

You'll notice that we're using transparent paper for our patterns. This type of paper makes finding the "perfect" grain for each section much easier. The transparent paper is available from us. We have 25" x 38" sheets available for $2.00 each and 17 ½" x 23" for $1.00 each.

If you can find a copy shop that will make copies in a color other than black, it will be much easier to see where your blade is at all times. Sometimes the dark blade gets lost in the black line. Drifting from one side to the other, even on a thin line, can make a difference in making the parts fit accurately.

We have also made 3D images of the projects in this book available on our website. You can click on the images and view them from different angles. Visit **www.intarsia.com** for more information.

Photo 2.2. The pattern's parts are cut up and ready to be glued to the wood.

Step 4 The beak and the light-colored areas (*LT*) could use some extra detail provided by unusual grain patterns or by wood that goes from a lighter shade to a darker shade toward the lower portion of the beak. Choose appropriate wood for these sections (See the tip box on page 20 for more information).

Step 5 Mark the five pattern parts that you can get out of one pattern (see Photo 2.1). Use a series of arrows to mark the outside edges of the piece (see **Photo 2.2**).

Step 6 The nostril and the pupil can be cut out and inlaid, or you can use a woodburner to define the parts. If you going to inlay the parts, drill in the center of the cut-out area and thread your scroll saw blade through the hole. If you are woodburning, you will burn these areas after the parts have been shaped.

Photo 2.3. Cut the outside edges first to get into the swing of sawing.

Photo 2.4. Use a #5 blade to cut around the outside; then use a #1 or a #2 to slice up the parts.

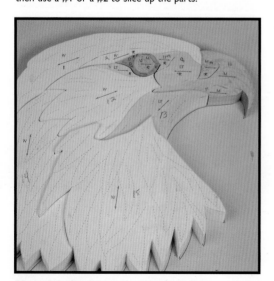

Photo 2.5. Check how everything fits before removing the paper.

Sawing the Bald Eagle

Step 7 Begin cutting. For this Bald Eagle project, you could start sawing just about anywhere you would like. If you are going to start sawing the white wood first, saw all of the white wood and then saw the softer western red cedar so you don't have to keep switching blades (see A Word About Scroll Saw Blades on page 8).

Step 8 Saw the outside areas of the project first (see **Photo 2.3**). The outside edges don't have to fit next to other parts, so you don't have to worry if you drift off the line. For this piece, we used a #7 blade and started sawing on the two neck parts: the large one on the right side and the left one that adjoins it.

Step 9 After sawing the two parts of the neck, leave them together.

Step 10 Once all of the white parts are cut, change to a #5 blade and cut the rest of the head. Once you have sawn all of the colors, slice up the different parts using a #1 or a #2 blade (see **Photo 2.4**).

Step 11 After all of the parts have been cut, turn each part over to the backside and remove any burr or tear out. Transfer the number of the piece from the front to the back.

Checking for fit

Step 12 Before taking the paper off, look over the project to see if everything is fitting alright (see **Photo 2.5**). Any line work that shows on the pattern may reveal a problem with the fit. If there is a fit problem, mark any parts and trim them with the saw. Use a new, sharp blade to trim any parts. Re-cut any parts as necessary.

Sanding and shaping

Step 13 When you are satisfied with the fit, remove the paper. Make a sanding shim for the entire head and a separate one for the beak (see **Photo 2.6**).

Step 14 The first part/parts you sand will determine how much dimension your project will have. The Bald Eagle doesn't have a background-type part to sand first, so we will start by sanding the head area, using the sanding shim. If you can locate some books with eagle head pictures, it will be helpful to have them nearby as a reference.

Step 15 Turn all of the parts—except the eye and eyebrow parts—upside down and use double-sided carpet tape to secure the parts to the sanding shims (see **Photo 2.7**). Use at least two pieces of tape to hold each part down. It is easier to put the tape on the backsides of the parts, as opposed to putting the tape on the sanding shims. When you are working with more than one area taped to a sanding shim, tape up both sections together as shown (see **Photo 2.8**).

Step 16 Start thinning the neck area. Use a pencil to mark the areas you want to sand on the face of the wood (see **Photo 2.9**). The more clues you give yourself at the sander, the better off you will be.

Step 17 After you lower the neck area down to about ½" thick, start tapering the face area down toward the beak. The corner where the beak almost reaches the center of the eye should be a little thicker than the facial part surrounding it. To create this effect, taper the face down so that the beak will be a little thicker.

Step 18 Angle the top of the head from the eye area up toward the top outer edge. Any parts angled this way will catch more light and make the project look more dimensional.

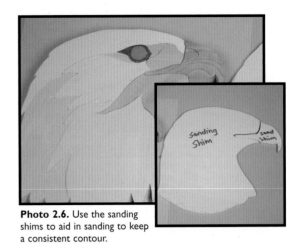

Photo 2.6. Use the sanding shims to aid in sanding to keep a consistent contour.

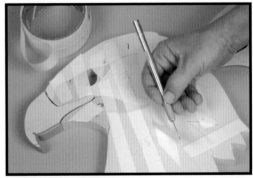

Photo 2.7. Use double-sided tape to secure the parts to the sanding shims.

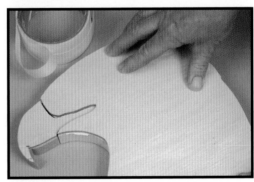

Photo 2.8. Tape both the head sections and beak sections to their sanding shims, carefully lining them up so that you are able to put the beak back in place while it is still taped to the sanding shim.

Photo 2.9. Mark the surface of the areas to be sanded; the head is first, then the beak.

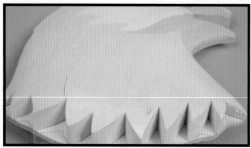

Photo 2.10. Lower the neck area, round the sides and the top of the head, and leave the bottom area thick.

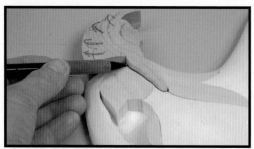

Photo 2.11. Mark where the face joins the beak on the upper part.

Photo 2.12. Mark where the face joins the beak on the lower part.

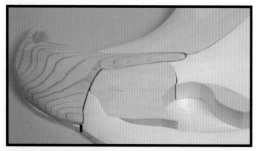

Photo 2.13. The upper beak is roughed in. Note how the grain pattern changed.

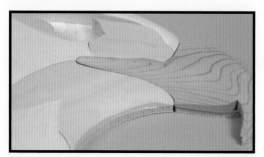

Photo 2.14. Notice how the lower beak is a little thicker than the face area.

Step 19 Round the sides of the Bald Eagle's face. Leave the area along the bottom thick. Our theory is that whenever a project has a section missing or cut off (like the body portion below the head on the Bald Eagle) we leave that area thick, as if it were just removed from the body part. We round natural-ending outside edges (like the sides and top of the Bald Eagle's head) all the way down to the outside edge (see **Photo 2.10**).

Step 20 Rough in the beak. Put the beak in place and use a pencil to mark the thickness of the face area that joins the beak (see **Photos 2.11** and **2.12**). As you sand these sections, be sure that you can see your pencil line. If you sand below the pencil line, you will need to mark the face area and sand it down again until it is thinner than the beak. Remember to guard against the cycle of sanding the face down, then sanding too much off the beak, then sanding the face down some more. Watch your pencil lines and try to stay above them.

Step 21 Sand the beak following the same contour as the face. Sand down just a little above the pencil line all around the beak. Sand the lower portion of the beak that cuts into the Bald Eagle's head, staying above the pencil line. The beak is narrow along the top edge and gets wider, like a triangle, down toward the lower portion of the beak. **Photos 2.13** and **2.14** show how much wood was removed from the face where it joins the beak. Also, the more you sand dips and rounded areas on the wood, the more the grain pattern will start to take on a life of its own.

Step 22 Now that all of the taped parts have been sanded and the face and beak match up, put the eye parts back in and mark around them (see **Photos 2.15** and **2.16**). Sand the dark outline parts down to the pencil line. Then, mark the eyeball, and round it down just below the pencil line. The eye will look better if it is sanded more like a dome rather than a half-ball shape; it will look "bug-eyed" if sanded too round.

Step 23 After the eye parts are sanded (see **Photos 2.17** and **2.18**), mark where these freshly sanded parts join the lower part of the brow. Sand the brow, staying about ⅟₃₂" to ⅟₁₆" above the pencil lines. After the eye is shaped, you can mark the pupil if you do not inlay this section.

TIP: A pallet knife or a thin chisel works great for prying parts off the sanding shim, but use caution because the tool can dent the bottom edge of a piece. If possible, we always pry from a side that will not have an exposed edge so that there aren't any dents showing. Sometimes we'll slide the tool in and barely pry the parts; then, we'll move around the parts to loosen the whole section rather than each individual part. On the Bald Eagle, we started prying the section as shown in the illustration.

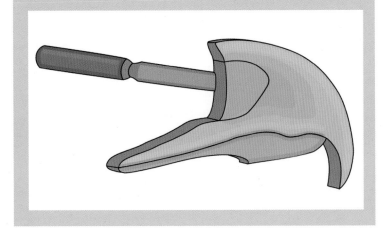

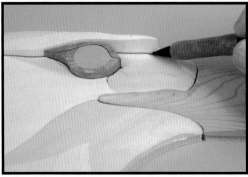

Photo 2.15. Mark with a pencil where the face joins the eye and brow parts.

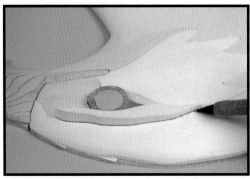

Photo 2.16. Mark both sides. When sanding these parts, stay above these lines.

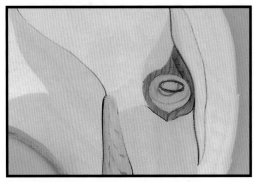

Photo 2.17. This side view shows the domelike shape of the eyeball.

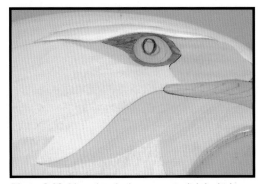

Photo 2.18. Note that the brow area is slightly thicker than the rest of the Bald Eagle.

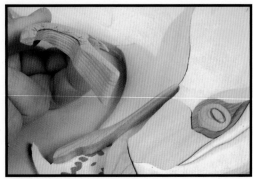

Photo 2.19. Mark how much you are going to sand off. This mark will give you a target line.

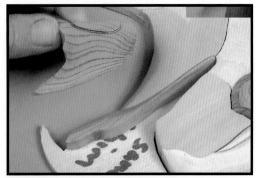

Photo 2.20. Note that the beak part that joins the face is slightly thicker than the face.

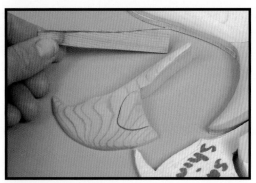

Photo 2.21. Mark the lower beak portion and sand down to that pencil line.

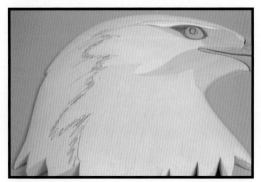

Photo 2.22. Mark the surface of the wood where you plan to sand.

Step 24 Start taking the parts off the sanding shim and adding more detail (See the tip box on page 25 for information on taking parts off the sanding shims). Take the upper beak part off the sanding shim; then, taper the beak down about 1⁄16" toward the face. The goal is to lower the larger beak section so the part closest to the face (the part with the nostril) will be slightly thicker than the rest of the beak. We mark a line to sand down to; that way, we can sand off a precisely even amount (see **Photo 2.19**).

Step 25 Put the beak back in place and mark around the beak part next to the face (see **Photo 2.20**). With the sander or by hand, bevel the edges down to this pencil line. The nostril will be detailed with a woodburner at a later time.

Step 26 The upper part of the beak overlaps the lower portion. To achieve this effect, make the lower beak a little thinner. Draw a line about 1⁄16" down from the surface, along the inside edge of the lower beak. Taper down to this pencil line, tapering from the edge that joins the neck section down to the 1⁄16" pencil line (see **Photo 2.21**). Do not sand where the lower beak joins the *LT* section of the neck.

Step 27 The beak should be a little thicker than the facial area surrounding the beak. If you sand below the pencil lines on the beak indicating the thickness of the parts around it, you will have to sand the parts down to match the new thickness line. Slightly round the upper beak portion down to the pencil line. Start taking the rest of the parts off the sanding shim.

Step 28 We'll be tapering the left side of the neck part down toward the adjoining neck part, rather than sanding down the entire surface of the part. Mark the surface of the wood where you will be sanding (see **Photo 2.22**). Then, take that part out and mark the edge about 1⁄16" down from the top, using the penciled area on the surface as a guide for where to start and stop the line. Sand down to the pencil line (see **Photo 2.23**). Taper to blend this area in rather than just rolling the edge down toward the 1⁄16" pencil line. The goal is to try to give the feathering some layers.

Step 29 After sanding, put the part back in place and mark the position of any adjoining parts. Next, work the top of the head part. We will be matching the top head part to the left neck section that was just sanded. The goal is to match up the two sections so the feathers will look like they are overlapping (see **Photo 2.24**). They do not have to match perfectly; a little variation will add to the feathering effect.

Step 30 After both sections are sanded and marked, make a small chamfer down to the pencil line to soften the hard edge (see **Photo 2.25**).

Step 31 Lower the part under the cheek area to make it look like the feathers are overlapping (see **Photo 2.26**). As before, mark the area on the surface and the edge before sanding. Note the area marked in the photo. Do not sand much off the left side of this part; that edge is overlapping the outside part.

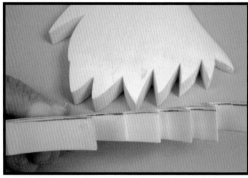

Photo 2.23. Mark 1/16" down on the edge of the part you plan on sanding.

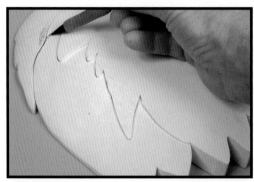

Photo 2.24. Mark where the left neck part joins the top head part. Sand the top head part down to this pencil line.

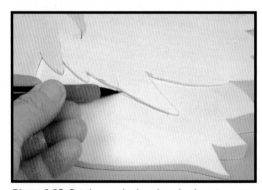

Photo 2.25. Put the part back and mark where it meets the next part.

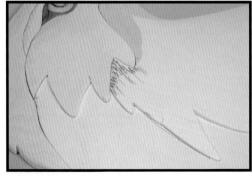

Photo 2.26. Mark the surface of the next area to be sanded. Lower this part.

Photo 2.27. Mark the areas to be burned and the lines to follow for texture.

Photo 2.28. Texture lines are marked all over the piece as a guide for the Wonder Wheel.

Photo 2.29. A tool called the Wonder Wheel is ideal for adding texture to intarsia projects.

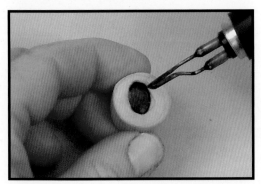

Photo 2.30. Knifelike woodburning tips work great for lines and shading.

Adding Texture

Step 32 Using the pattern as a guide, mark the areas that will be burned and the lines to follow if you are adding texture to the Bald Eagle. We draw pencil lines to guide me as we apply a featherlike texture (see **Photos 2.27** and **2.28**). The Bald Eagle also looks fine without texture.

Step 33 Use the Wonder Wheel or a V-shaped carving tool to gouge out the texture. If you are using aspen, do not use much pressure as you press the wood against the wheel (see **Photo 2.29**). The more pressure, the deeper and more burned the grooves will be. Do not make the texture too dark on the Bald Eagle; applying lots of pressure to the white wood can make the burnished areas look dirty.

Step 34 Texture all the way down the outside edges to give the project even more dimension. Use a combination of ¾"- to ¼"-long strokes. Make these lines somewhat sporadic rather than evenly lined and spaced. Avoid crisscrossing the lines or making X or + lines because they do not look natural. If you aren't yet comfortable using the wheel, get some scrap wood out and practice putting texture on it before you texture your project.

Step 35 Use a pencil to mark the nostril and the pupil if you did not inlay them. We find it best to use a knifelike burning tip to do any detail. Make the outer curved line cut through the grain like a knife (see **Photo 2.30**). Then, put the burning tip on its side to shade the rest of the pupil. Draw pupils on some scrap wood and practice before burning the actual part. The same applies to the nostril.

Hand sanding and detailing

Step 36 After texturing all of the parts, lightly hand sand the surface of each part. Soften the edges by slightly rounding them. Don't round too much between the parts or you'll take away from the overall appearance of the project. Over-rounding will make your project look like a quilt—your eye will see the parts first, then the picture.

Step 37 The areas between the upper and lower beak and around the eyebrow may need heavy rounding. If deep scratches are visible, sand the parts using 180-grit sandpaper, sanding with the grain. Then, use 220-grit sandpaper for the final hand sanding. Erase any pencil lines that may be showing.

Step 38 Add the highlight to the eye. Start by marking the location of the highlight with typewriter correction fluid (see **Photo 2.31**).

Step 39 Use a small dowel made out of aspen for the highlight in the eye. To make the dowel, cut pieces of aspen close to the size of a pencil. Then, use a pencil sharpener to shape/round both ends of the aspen pieces. The cone shape that the pencil sharpener makes works well for any size hole drilled for highlights.

Step 40 Drill a small hole where you want the highlight, cut the end off the aspen, put a little glue in the hole, and then place the cone-shaped dowel in the hole (see **Photo 2.32**). Press tightly, and wait a few minutes for the glue to dry.

Step 41 After the glue is dry, sand the highlight flush with the rest of the eye. This highlight is in lighter-colored wood, and it will not show up as much as it does on the darker wood; however, when the finish is applied, it will have more contrast. Notice the difference between the burned pupil and the inlaid pupil (see **Photo 2.33**). The inlaid pupil will have more contrast once the finish is applied. The Bald Eagle is ready for a finish (see **Photo 2.34**).

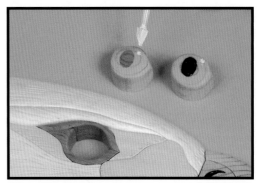

Photo 2.31. You can use a white correction fluid to mark the highlight of the eye.

Photo 2.32. Make a small cone, using a pencil sharpener, for the highlight.

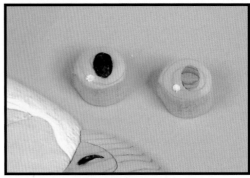

Photo 2.33. Sand the highlight flush with the eye.

Photo 2.34. The Bald Eagle is ready for finishing. It looks "soft" at this point.

Photo 2.35. Use a terry cloth rag to help remove gel from the texture.

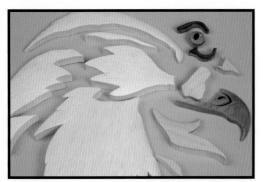

Photo 2.36. All parts have one coat of gel. Let them dry overnight.

Photo 2.37. Use the project to trace the backing pattern.

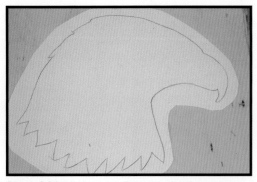

Photo 2.38. Use a spray adhesive to glue the paper on the plywood. When you cut the pattern, stay $\frac{1}{32}$" to $\frac{1}{16}$" inside the line.

Applying the finish

Step 42 Apply finish to each of the parts and allow the first coat to dry overnight to make sure it has dried thoroughly (see **Photo 2.35**).

Step 43 If you applied texture to the Bald Eagle, use a lint-free terry cloth towel to wipe off the gel (see **Photo 2.36**). With a little pressure, the terry cloth will get the excess gel out of the grooves. For any parts that have sharp inside corners, consider blowing out these areas with compressed air, which liquefies the gel. Be sure to check the tops of the parts for any gel that may have run onto the surface and wipe these areas immediately.

Step 44 The second coat can be applied the same way as the first coat, except we do not coat all of the edges. Only coat the edges that are exposed around the outside of the project and all surfaces for the second coat.

Step 45 After four to six hours, apply the third and final coat. The gel works very well with cedar and does not raise the grain, so there is no need to sand or use steel wool between coats. The gel will raise the grain slightly on white woods like aspen and white pine, so use #0000 steel wool lightly before applying the third coat. We used the steel wool on all of the white Bald Eagle parts. After the third coat dries (in about four hours) the project can be assembled.

Make the backing

Step 46 Use ¼" luan plywood, and trace around the actual parts to create a pattern for the backing (see **Photo 2.37**).

Step 47 Stay to the inside of the line, about $\frac{1}{32}$" to $\frac{1}{16}$", when you cut the backing (see **Photo 2.38**). This will make the backing a little smaller than the project.

Step 48 Stain the edges with a dark brown leather dye; then sand the back and the edges. Assemble the parts on the backing to check the fit.

Glue the Bald Eagle down

Step 49 Before you begin gluing, look at the placement on the backing for optimum fit. Carefully pick up the one part that will help to "lock the project in." In this case, the larger white part would be a great part to lock in the project. This part is large enough to accommodate both the hot melt glue and the yellow wood glue (see **Photo 2.39**). The hot melt glue acts as a clamp until the yellow wood glue dries.

Step 50 Put small dots of the yellow wood glue on first, leaving space between the dots for the hot melt glue. Check the project and get another view of its final position. Then, with a plan in mind, move as quickly as possible once you put the hot melt glue on. Press the part firmly in place. Hold it for about 15 seconds without moving it.

Step 51 Moving around to the other side, choose the top white part as the second piece to glue down. Glue this part using the same technique. With these two parts locked in place, use just dots of the yellow wood glue on the rest of the parts.

Step 52 Allow the glue to set before putting on the hanger (see **Photo 2.40** and the "Installing the Hanger" section on page 15 in Chapter One, for more information on installing the hardware).

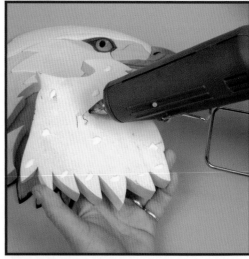

Photo 2.39. Use a combination of hot glue and yellow wood glue. The hot glue works like a clamp as the yellow glue dries.

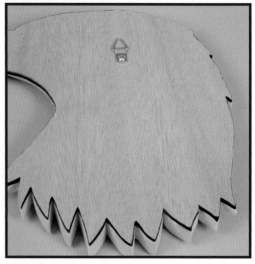

Photo 2.40. Apply a mirror hanger very neatly to the back of the project.

TIP: Use a sponge brush to apply the leather dye to the edges of the plywood backing after it has been cut out. It is a good idea to wear some rubber gloves, as the leather dye may also dye your skin. If you use material like tempered masonite for the backing, you will not need to stain the edges because it is already very dark. After the dye is dry, spray the sides and the backside of the backing—whether it's plywood or masonite—with a clear acrylic spray to help seal in the project.

Wild Mustang Demonstration

Tools
- ■ Scroll saw (or band saw)
- ■ Sander for contouring
- ■ Drill
- ■ Carving or X-Acto knife
- ■ Woodburner (optional)

Wood
- ■ Dark shade at least 3" wide by 2" long and ¾" thick
- ■ Medium-dark shade at least 3" wide by 3" long and ¾" thick
- ■ Medium shade at least 5" wide by 6" long and ¾" thick
- ■ Light shade at least 7" wide by 18" long and ¾" thick
- ■ White shade at least 6" wide by 24" long and ¾" thick
- ■ ¼" luan plywood for the backing

Materials
- ■ Glue stick or spray adhesive, repositionable
- ■ Five copies of the Wild Mustang pattern
- ■ Yellow wood glue
- ■ Double-sided tape
- ■ Hot melt glue and glue gun
- ■ Polyurethane wiping gel or finish of choice
- ■ Paper towels
- ■ 1" disposable foam brush
- ■ Brown leather dye
- ■ Clear acrylic spray
- ■ Mirror hanger or hanger of choice

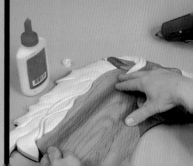

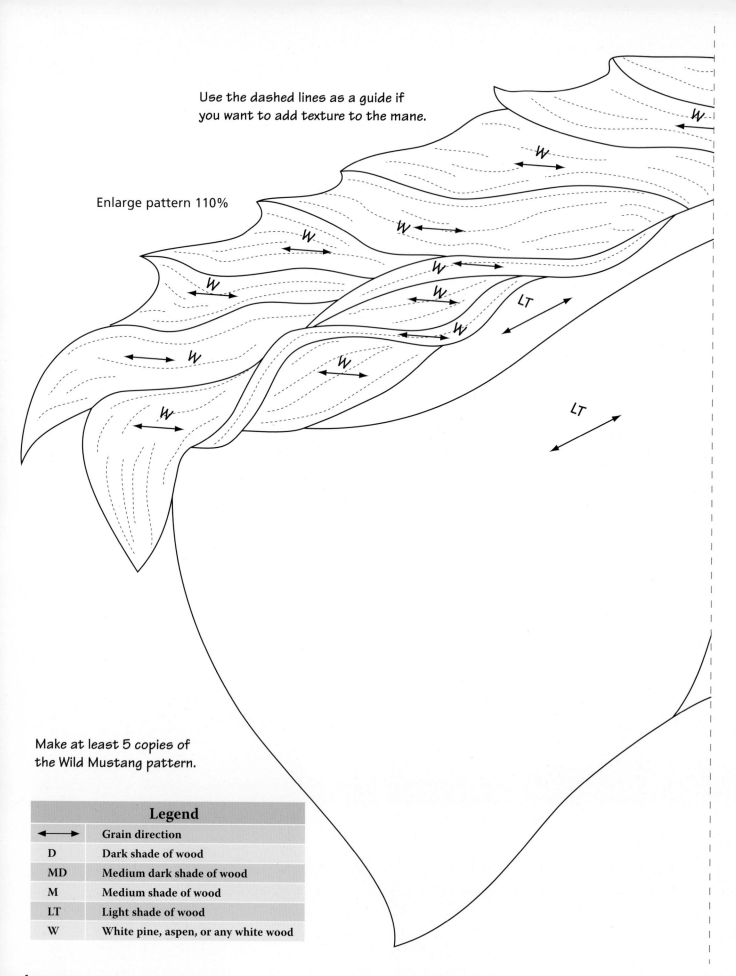

Use the dashed lines as a guide if
you want to add texture to the mane.

Enlarge pattern 110%

Make at least 5 copies of
the Wild Mustang pattern.

Legend	
←——→	**Grain direction**
D	**Dark shade of wood**
MD	**Medium dark shade of wood**
M	**Medium shade of wood**
LT	**Light shade of wood**
W	**White pine, aspen, or any white wood**

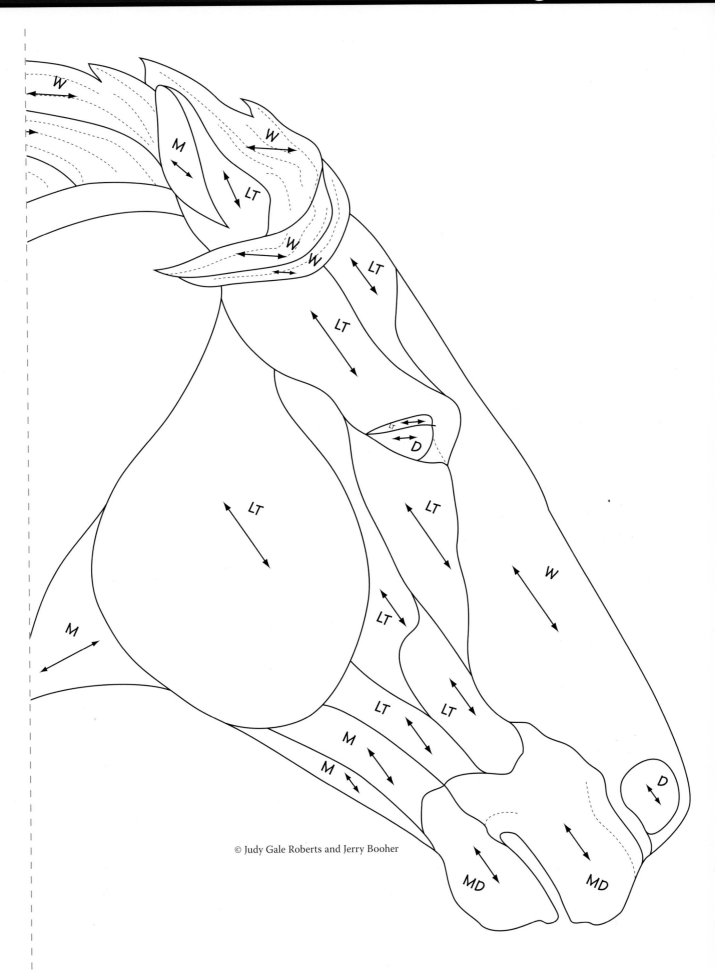

© Judy Gale Roberts and Jerry Booher

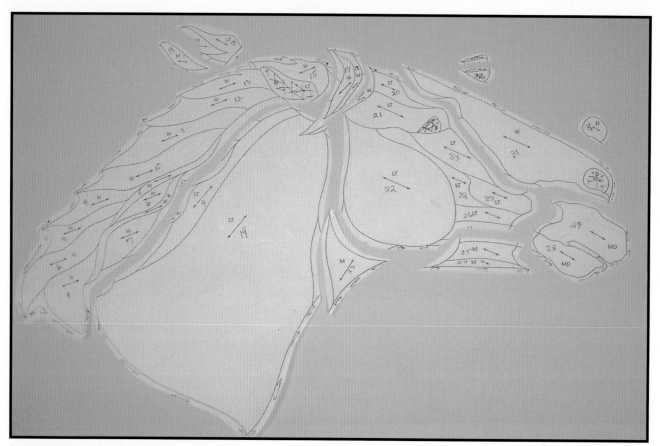

Photo 3.1. Cut up the pattern. Note the sections that can stay as one pattern section. If the color and grain direction is the same, leave those parts together.

TIP: The Wild Mustang is a very versatile pattern as far as coloring goes. You can use whatever color combinations you like, depending on what wood you have available.

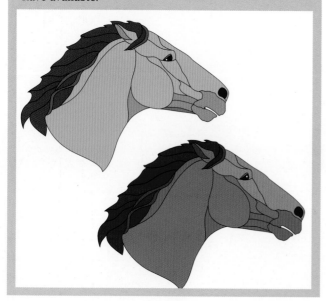

Pattern preparation and layout

Step 1 Glance over the pattern. The mane, face, and neck areas can be cut in sections rather than cutting each part from a different pattern. If you have wood that is wide enough, lay out the entire *W* mane in one section and the two *LT* neck parts in one section.

Step 2 Make at least five photocopies of the pattern. Label one of the pattern copies as the master copy and number each part on the master.

Step 3 Cut out each section from the photocopies, leaving about a ¼" border around the line work (see **Photo 3.1**).

Step 4 Glue the pattern to the wood with a temporary adhesive. Trim any excess paper even with the edge of the board and mark the outside edges of the pattern.

Scroll sawing

Step 5 Saw the outside areas of the project first. We used a #5 blade to make all of the outside cuts.

Step 6 Once all of the sections have been cut, use a smaller blade, such as a #1 or a #2, to separate the individual parts.

Step 7 If you are going to inlay the dark nostril part, drill a hole and thread your blade through the hole to cut out the area.

Step 8 Remove the burr before checking the fit. If this is not done before checking the fit, you may get a false reading and trim some parts that may not need to be trimmed.

Checking for fit

Step 9 Before taking the paper off, check the overall project to see if everything is fitting correctly (see **Photo 3.2**). If there are heavy pattern lines on both parts, you may need to trim closer to the line, removing most of the line with a very sharp, new blade.

Step 10 Transfer the number from the pattern to the backside of the part (see **Photo 3.3**). When you are satisfied with the fit, remove the paper.

Sanding and shaping

Step 11 Take a minute and study the project (see **Photo 3.4**). Because some of the areas on this Wild Mustang will look better if they are sanded together to make the contour consistent, we'll need to make sanding shims later on.

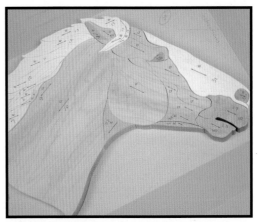

Photo 3.2. Leave the paper on the parts until you are satisfied with the fit.

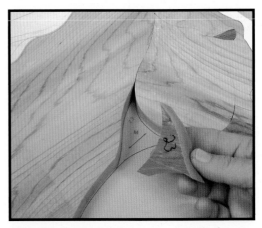

Photo 3.3. Transfer the number onto the back of each part.

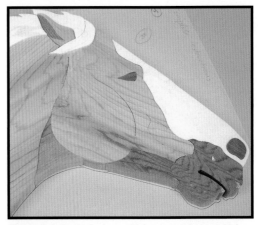

Photo 3.4. Study the horse. Make a mental note which parts to sand first.

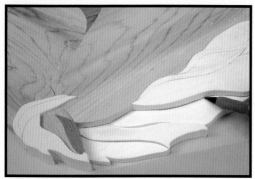

Photo 3.5. Start by sanding the mane. Work your way down, starting under the ear.

Photo 3.6. This line is made by marking the adjoining part.

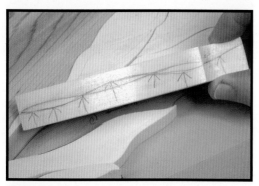

Photo 3.7. Mark dips opposite the pencil line.

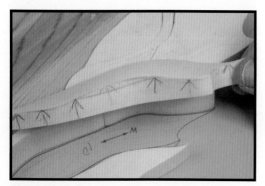

Photo 3.8. Sand down to the line with the arrows.

Step 12 As always, start with the parts that are in the background, or the parts that are the farthest from the viewer. On the Wild Mustang, most of the mane parts are farthest from the viewer, although a few mane parts will be in front of the neck and ear areas. Start with the mane section behind the ear and taper it down toward the Wild Mustang's neck to around ¼" where it joins the neck (see **Photo 3.5**). Sand some dips in the mane to give it a flowing feel.

Step 13 Mark where this mane section joins the parts around it. Each part will taper down toward the neck to give the neck some dimension.

Step 14 To add more interest to the mane, sand some dips in different places on each, or some, of the mane sections (see **Photo 3.6**). You can start with the first part of the mane behind the ear and sand a couple of dips into the surface.

Step 15 Put it back in place and mark where it joins the next mane section. Take the next mane section out and mark some opposite curved/dipped lines on the side of the part (see **Photo 3.7**). If there are too many lines and you get confused as to which one to sand, add some arrows to make it easier to follow the marks (see **Photo 3.8**). Even a slight variance in each part will catch the light and give the mane some movement.

Step 16 Work your way down the mane, marking and roughing in each part (see **Photo 3.9**). Some of these parts will be thicker to make these sections look like they are lying on top of the rest of the mane (see **Photo 3.10**).

Step 17 After you have sanded most of the mane, mark where these parts join the overlapping parts. Sand the overlapping parts, staying above the pencil line.

Step 18 Mark where the mane joins the neck (see **Photo 3.11**).

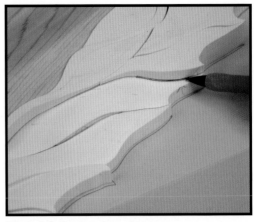

Photo 3.9. Continue down the mane.

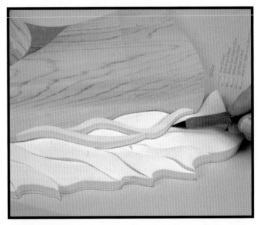

Photo 3.10. Sand the strandlike parts last. Stay above the pencil lines.

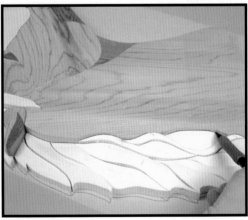

Photo 3.11. Mark where the mane joins the neck.

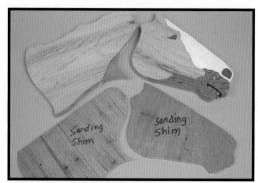

Photo 3.12. Use sanding shims to help sand a consistent contour.

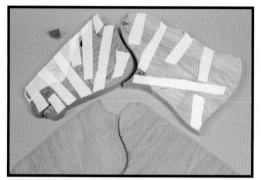

Photo 3.13. Use double-sided carpet tape to hold the parts in place.

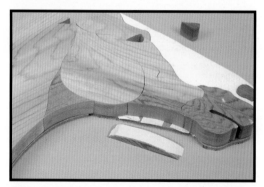

Photo 3.14. Edge-tape the lower part under the cheek.

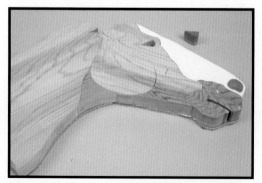

Photo 3.15. The taped sections should line up together to make it easier to match them up while sanding.

Step 19 Two sanding shims are needed to sand the horse (see **Photo 3.12**). The sanding shims help to create sections with a uniform contour. Trace around the parts on some plywood to create the patterns for the sanding shims. Make sure the plywood you use for the sanding shims is flat.

Step 20 Before you tape any of the parts, make sure you have marked where the mane joins the rest of the head and neck. Take the eye and eyelid out; do not sand these with the rest of the head. Turn all of the neck and head parts upside down and put strips of double-sided tape on the back of the wood (see **Photo 3.13**). Place the sanding shims on the taped parts; then carefully turn the taped sections over.

Step 21 Adjust any parts that may have moved as you turned the section over. We noticed, for instance, that the lower part next to the jaw could come off the sanding shim fairly easily. In cases like this, take the part off the sanding shim and put some double-sided tape between the parts to give it a little extra staying power (see **Photo 3.14**). When using these sanding shims, try to keep the shim even on the edge where the neck and head join. Making sure the sections line up will make sanding them to match much easier (see **Photo 3.15**).

TIP: When we make sanding shims, we also check to see if any parts can be raised to give the project more dimension. At this time, we do not see any parts that could be raised to make the Wild Mustang more dimensional. The ear could be raised; however, we'll sand the parts around it first and then decide if we need to raise it. Sometimes we will cut shims for raising sections and not use them, or we'll add shims after the fact. We like to have the sanding shims cut out prior to shaping the project so we won't have to break the rhythm to cut shims in the middle of sanding.

Step 22 Sand the neck, tapering it toward the head. If you have some pictures of horses, now would be a good time to have them to look at. The neck gets thinner toward the horse's head. Plus, by lowering the neck, it will make the prominent jaw stand out even more. Mark on the side how much wood to remove. We marked a line about half of the thickness. Tapering the neck down to around ⅜" will make the jaw/cheek and the head stand out much more. Make this a gradual taper rather than an abrupt drop to the ⅜" (see **Photo 3.16**).

Step 23 After sanding the taper, round the underside of the neck. Because there are no parts that join this area, you can round it all the way down the outside edge.

Step 24 Round the upper side of the neck, contouring it down to the pencil line that shows the thickness of the mane (see **Photo 3.17**). Sand the same contour all the way down. You need to lower and round the outside edge down toward the parts of the mane that look like they are lying on top of the neck. Remember, you are roughing in everything first; do not get too carried away "getting it perfect."

Step 25 Put the neck section next to the head and mark where it joins the head (see **Photo 3.18**).

Step 26 Rough in the head section. The eye area will be the thickest part of the face. Taper the head, starting just below the eye. Sand down toward the nose, tapering it down to around ½" for now.

Step 27 Taper from the eye (the high point),and sand down toward the ear. The parts above the eye will need to be lower than the parts of the mane/forelock to make it look as though the mane is on top of that area. We found it easier to get these two angles first, and then come back and sand, starting with the eye as the high point again and tapering down toward the bottom edge of the face.

Step 28 Taper from the eye down along the front of the face. We marked a circular area that we will stay away from initially. The arrows show which direction the taper will go (see **Photo 3.19**).

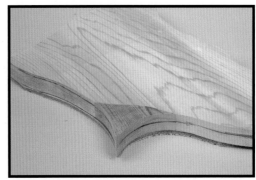
Photo 3.16. Give yourself a line to sand down to, about half the thickness.

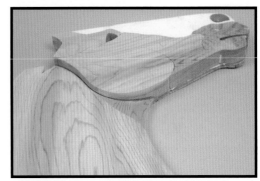
Photo 3.17. After sanding the taper, round the sides.

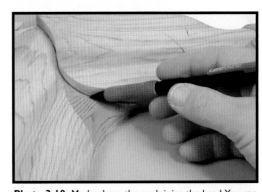
Photo 3.18. Mark where the neck joins the head. You can see from the picture how much was sanded off the neck.

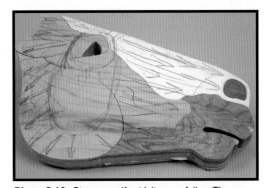
Photo 3.19. Give yourself guidelines to follow. The eye area will be the thickest. Every part will taper down from the eye.

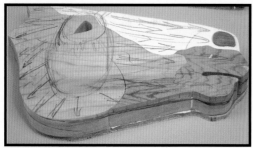

Photo 3.20. Note the sides showing how much we plan on removing.

Photo 3.21. Notice that the eye area is the thickest in this side view after sanding.

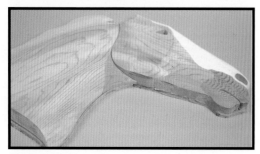

Photo 3.22. The head is in place after sanding the first taper.

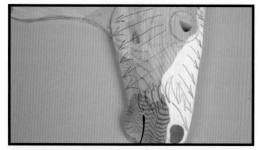

Photo 3.23. Next, taper from the eye down to the lower outside edge, then from the eye to the top outside edge.

Photo 3.24. The head is in place after sanding the second angle.

Step 29 Taper the cheek down toward the pencil line showing the thicknesses of the neck. Stay ¹⁄₁₆" above the pencil line for now (see **Photos 3.20**, **3.21**, and **3.22**).

Step 30 With the upper and lower parts tapered, work on the underside of the head and the forehead section. Taking off from the eye again, sand down toward the outer sides, sanding the front/top of the face down toward the outer edge with more of a flat angle than a round contour. Do the same from below the eye and down toward the underside of the head (see **Photo 3.23**).

Step 31 After both sections have been roughed in, start taking some of the parts off the sanding shims to add more detail. Before taking anything off the sanding shims, make sure the neck and the head sections match up (see **Photo 3.24** and **Photo 3.25**).

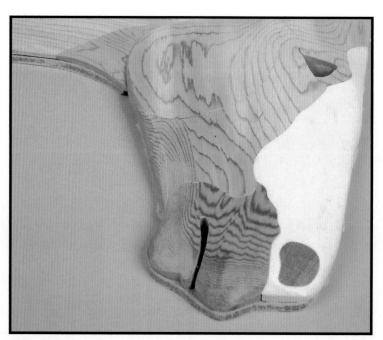

Photo 3.25. This photo shows the front view of the sanded areas.

Step 32 The next parts to rough in will be the ear and the mane, or forelock, that comes around in front of the ear. Mark around the ear and forelock (see **Photo 3.26**).

Step 33 Sand the ear first, and then mark where it joins the forelock.

Step 34 Taper the ear down to meet the thickness of the forelock. Leave the tip of the ear the full thickness. The ear is coming out from behind the forelock. Round the upper ear part down toward the top/outside edge.

Step 35 To give the ear more depth, taper the darker part down toward the inside of the ear (see **Photo 3.27**). This will give the ear more of a hollow look inside.

Step 36 Sand the mane/forelock parts, staying above all of the pencil lines (see **Photo 3.28**). Sand them down to around ¹⁄₁₆" above the pencil lines. Taper them down toward the outside edge to make them look like they are coming from behind and wrapping around the ear (see **Photo 3.29**). Sand both forelock parts the same. You can hold these two sections together and sand them at one time or use some double-sided tape to hold them together. Later we will add more definition between the two parts.

Step 37 When everything is close to the heights and shapes you want, go back to add more detail to each part. Leaving the forelock parts slightly thicker than the pencil line that shows the thickness of the forehead makes it look as though the forelock is lying on top of the head.

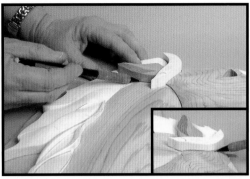

Photo 3.26. Mark the ear and the forelock/mane parts. Taper the ear in.

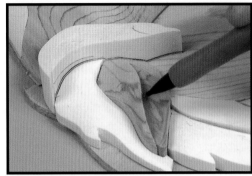

Photo 3.27. Taper the darker part down toward the inside of the ear.

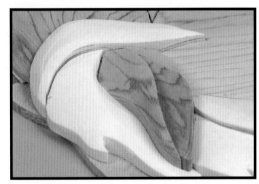

Photo 3.28. Sand the forelock, staying above the pencil line.

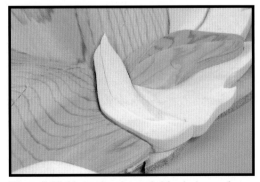

Photo 3.29. Notice that the sanded forelock, seen from this top view, is ¹⁄₁₆" thicker than the forehead, neck, and ear sections.

Photo 3.30. Realign the mane with the neck, marking between the two sections.

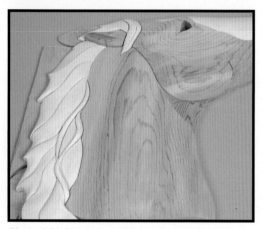

Photo 3.31. The mane and the neck are sanded before taking off the shim.

Step 38 Fine-tune a few areas before you start taking the pieces off the sanding shims. Using some scrap plywood, align the mane with the neck. Mark any areas that are higher than the neck (see **Photo 3.30**). Most of the mane should be thinner than the neck with the exception of the strandlike parts and some of the mane toward the end of the neck. If the neck is thicker than the mane where the mane should overlap it, sand the neck down before removing it from the sanding shim. The mane parts that appear to be overlapping the neck should be thicker than the neck. Round the edges of these overlapping parts (see **Photo 3.31**).

TIP: As you're working, try looking at your project from a distance. Because the project isn't glued down, we will either put it on the floor and look down at it or get up on a ladder and look at it on the floor. If it is something very critical, like a face, we will use double-sided tape and tape the whole project to a piece of plywood so that we can stand it up and see how the light is going to effect the appearance. Because intarsia projects are dimensional, it is important to view them from different angles.

Step 39 Now we want to make the jaw/cheek area prominent on the horse. To add this element, take the cheek part off the sanding shim. A pallet knife or a thin chisel works great for this task. If you have to pry any parts, don't wedge the chisel under an exposed area. It may dent the wood. Always pry from an edge that is not exposed.

Step 40 Mark the face of the wood where you want to remove material (see **Photo 3.32**). Also mark on the side so that you can see the lines as you sand down to them. Take off at least ¹⁄₁₆"; we sanded down about ⅛". Take off more toward the lower part of the face. The cheek will stick out more along the bottom edge. Taper these areas and blend the taper back into the rest of the face. Do not just round abruptly down to the line.

Step 41 Blend up to the muzzle area. The muzzle is a little thicker, so stay away from that area for now. After sanding, put the cheek back in place and mark where the face joins the cheek (see **Photo 3.33**). Note how the cheek is around ⅛" thick along the bottom side and only ¹⁄₁₆" thick just below the eye. Starting the taper about ½" from the edge, taper the cheek down to the pencil line. There is flesh that covers the face, so the cheek needs to blend in, leaving most of the height (see **Photo 3.34**).

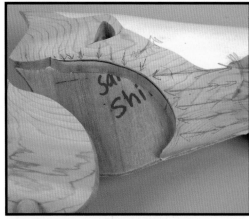

Photo 3.32. Take the cheek out and lower the adjoining parts.

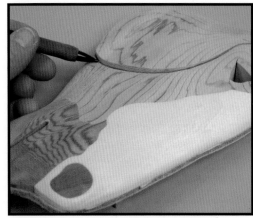

Photo 3.33. Mark where the face joins the cheek.

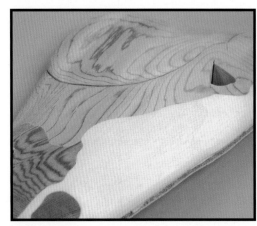

Photo 3.34. The cheek is in place after it was tapered to match the face.

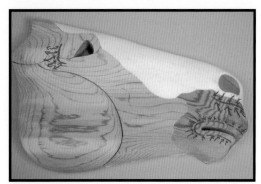

Photo 3.35. Mark the areas to be carved and sanded with more detail.

Photo 3.36. Lower the area inside the nostril and above the eyelid.

Photo 3.37. Mark an angled line to sand down to.

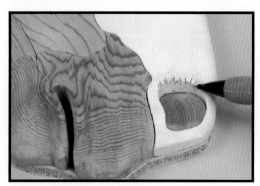

Photo 3.38. Soften by hand sanding the sharp edge.

Step 42 The eye area could use some more detail. Add a dip on the back of the eye area to make the eye stand out even more. Mark the surface of the wood where you want to sand the dip (see **Photo 3.35**). In the picture, the cheek is in place, but it's not taped in. When sanding, take the cheek out.

Step 43 The areas around the nose and the mouth could also use more detail. Use the Wonder Wheel to carve a crease line below the nostril to make the nostril flare out a little. To give the lips some detail, use the wheel to carve a groove around the mouth, and then blend the groove around the lip area. The lips will be higher, so remove the material around the lips however you can. (A knife also works well for these areas.)

Step 44 Next, we will be taking more parts off the sanding shim. Mark the area just above the eyelid and the inside corner of the eye. The eyelid will need to be a little thicker, and we have not removed much material around the eye. Just mark it for now.

Step 45 The nostril would look much better if we lowered it (see **Photo 3.36**). We leave the outside edge the same thickness and taper the dark part in toward the rest of the face. This helps to give the appearance of a hole that gets deeper as it goes into the head.

Step 46 Take all of the head parts off the sanding shim. Take the nostril part and mark an angled line, starting flush with the outer edge and down about ⅛" or more toward the inside edge (see **Photo 3.37**).

Step 47 After sanding, put the nostril part back. Hand round the edges of the white wood to soften the edge, which will make the nostril area look soft (see **Photo 3.38**).

Step 48 Moving back to the eye, start by carving down the inside corner of the eye, just in front of the dark eye part. Taper the part above the eyelid down a little in toward the eyelid, be sure to do that before putting the eye and lid in place. Mark around the eye and lid (see **Photo 3.39**).

Step 49 Sand the eye first. Sand it into more of a dome shape than a round ball shape. The more it looks like a round ball, the more bug-eyed it will look. Round the eye down to the pencil line showing the thickness of the corner of the eye.

Step 50 Put the eye back and mark the underside of the eyelid. Stay above all pencil lines on the lid. Depending on how much you sanded off around the eye, you may not be sanding much off the lid.

Step 51 Now that the parts are off the sanding shim, you can work with the individual parts around the mouth. Round the lips to the inside (see **Photo 3.40**). You can do this by hand or use your sander.

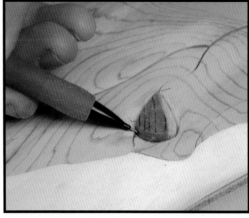

Photo 3.39. Mark around the eye and the eyelid.

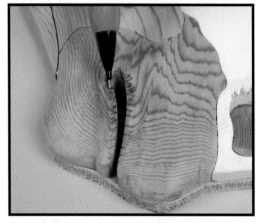

Photo 3.40. Soften the lips, either by hand or with a sander.

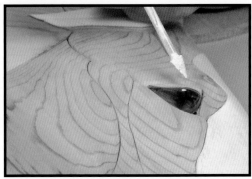

Photo 3.41. Mark the highlighted area with white.

Photo 3.42. Drill a small hole for the highlight.

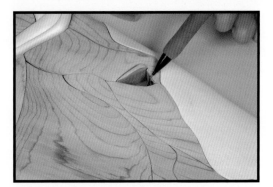

Photo 3.43. The corner of the eye can be carved or burned to add more detail.

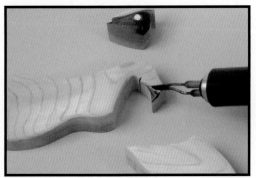

Photo 3.44. You can use a woodburner to add detail.

Step 52 Use the Wonder Wheel to burnish the eye; it will darken the wood and give it a nice sheen. You can also use a woodburner to darken the eye.

Step 53 To add the final touch to the eye, make a small dowel out of aspen for the highlight in the eye. Cut pieces of aspen close to the size of a pencil and use a pencil sharpener to shape the end of the dowel.

Step 54 Use some white typewriter correction fluid to mark the location of the highlight (see **Photo 3.41**). Drill a small hole where you want the highlight; We used a ¹⁄₁₆" drill bit (see **Photo 3.42**).

Step 55 Cut the end off the aspen and put a little glue in the hole; then, place the cone-shaped dowel in. Press tightly and wait a few minutes for the glue to dry.

Step 56 After the glue is dry, sand the dowel flush with the rest of the eye. Add some extra detail by darkening the corner of the eye with a woodburner (see **Photos 3.43** and **3.44**).

Step 57 Take the rib section of the neck off the sanding shim. We are going to add a little detail to give the neck some muscle. Mark a line about ⅛" down and sand the surface down to that mark (see **Photo 3.45**). Taper the part down to this pencil line, making sure it's blended in.

Step 58 Put the part back and mark the height of the riblike part that was just sanded (see **Photo 3.46**). Take the larger neck part and roll it down to the pencil line (see **Photo 3.47**).

Step 59 Before taking the other two parts of the neck off the sanding shim, hand sand the surface; if there are any deep scratches, sand those out either by hand or by using a sander. Take all of the parts off the neck sanding shim and reassemble the parts on the pattern.

Step 60 At this point, you could add a hairlike texture to the mane with the Wonder Wheel. We chose not to add texture to the mane because the dips we sanded would make it hard to get the Wonder Wheel down into the dips in a consistent manner. If you did not sand many dips in the mane, the hairlike texture would add a nice contrast to the smooth parts of the horse. Use the dashed lines on the pattern as a guide. Mark a few lines on each part to give you a general idea which way you want the lines to go.

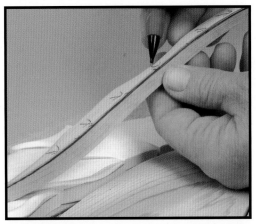

Photo 3.45. Mark about ⅛" down on the riblike section of the neck.

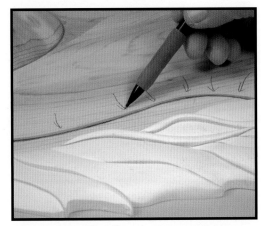

Photo 3.46. Round the larger neck portion down to meet the pencil line.

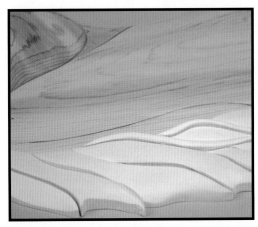

Photo 3.47. The neck is rounded down to meet the riblike section.

Photo 3.48. Hand sand each part. The Wild Mustang is ready for the finish.

TIP: For finish sanding, we only go up to a 220-grit paper. Wood that has been sanded with a very fine grit sandpaper may have trouble accepting the finish. We try to do most of our sanding with the sander (180 grit), sanding with the grain whenever possible. It is important to sand with the grain. Then, we use a smaller sander with a 220-grit sleeve to sand each part. This method speeds the "clean-up sanding" considerably.

Hand sand each part

Step 61 Go over each part. Hold it up to the light to see if there are any humps, bumps, or scratches. Hand sand the edges, barely knocking off the sharp corners on all parts (see **Photo 3.48**). Erase any pencil lines that may be showing, and check again for any deep scratches.

Applying the finish

Step 62 Dust or blow off all of the parts. Finish the Wild Mustang by referring back to the instructions for finishing the Bald Eagle in Chapter Two, page 30, and the "Applying the finish" section in Chapter One on page 13.

Make the backing

Step 63 After the finish has dried, create a backing for the piece from ¼" luan plywood. Refer to the instructions for making a backing in Chapter Two, page 30, and in Chapter One, page 14.

Glue the Wild Mustang down

Step 64 First, check the placement on the backing, going for optimum fit. Carefully pick up one of the parts that will help to "lock the project in." The larger neck section is a good choice, and it is large enough to accommodate both the hot melt glue and the yellow wood glue.

Step 65 Once you have applied the glue, move quickly and press the part firmly in place. Hold it for about 15 seconds without moving it (see **Photo 3.49**).

Step 66 Moving around to the other side, lock the blaze part in place with yellow wood glue and hot melt glue. The rest of the Wild Mustang can be glued using only the slower-setting yellow wood glue. Allow the glue to set before putting on the hanger. (Refer to the "Installing the Hanger" section in Chapter One on page 15 for more instructions.)

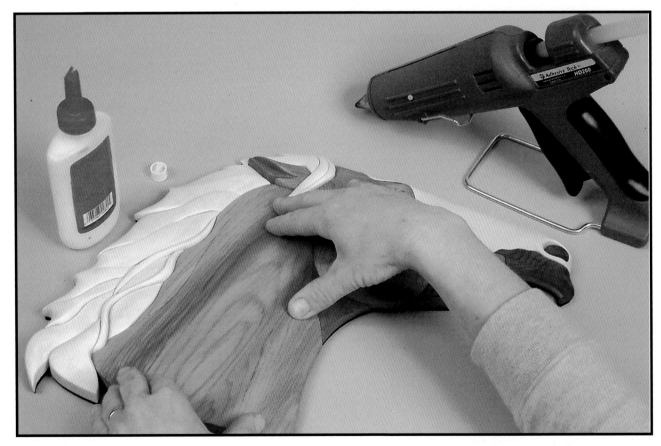

Photo 3.49. The white blaze and the larger neck part are good candidates to lock in the rest of the piece.

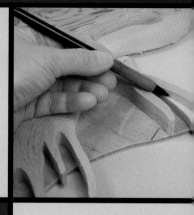

Bull Moose Demonstration

Tools
- ■ Scroll saw (or band saw)
- ■ Sander for contouring
- ■ Drill
- ■ Carving or X-Acto knife
- ■ Woodburner (optional)

Wood
- ■ Dark shade of wood at least 4" wide by 6" long and ¾" thick
- ■ Medium-dark shade of wood at least 7 ½" wide by 24" long and ¾" thick
- ■ Medium shade of wood at least 5" wide by 12" long and ¾" thick
- ■ Medium-light shade of wood at least 5" wide by 12" long and ¾" thick
- ■ ¼" luan plywood for the backing and sanding shim

Materials
- ■ Temporary adhesive (glue stick or spray)
- ■ At least six copies of the Bull Moose pattern
- ■ Yellow wood glue
- ■ Double-sided tape
- ■ Hot melt glue and glue gun
- ■ Polyurethane wiping gel or finish of choice
- ■ Paper towels
- ■ Lint-free terry cloth towel
- ■ 1" disposable foam brush
- ■ Brown leather dye
- ■ Clear acrylic spray
- ■ Mirror hanger or hanger of choice

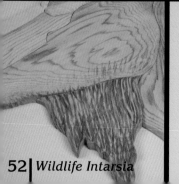

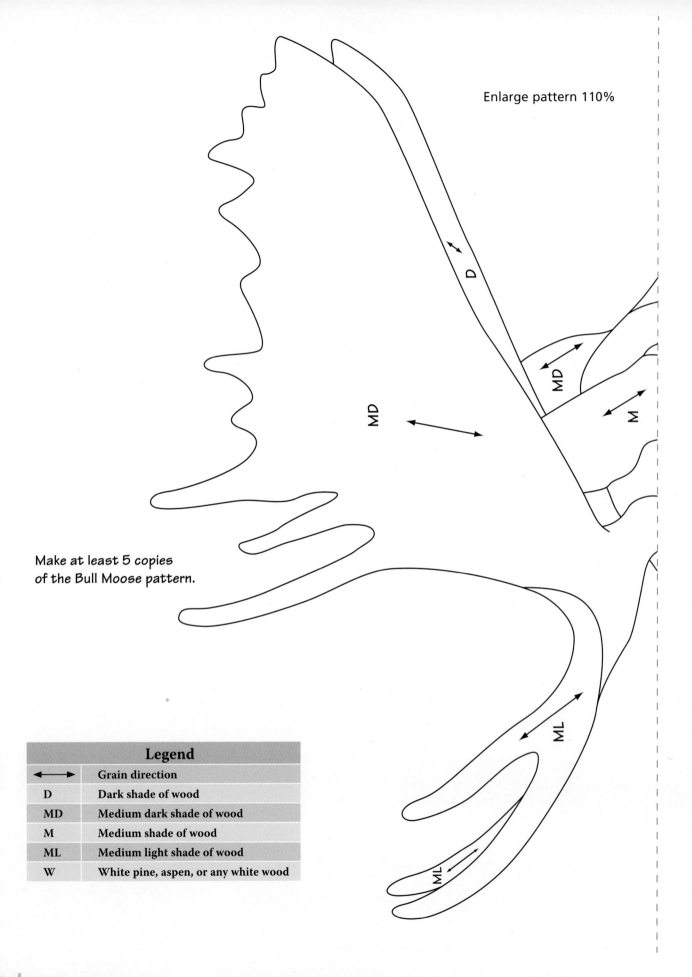

Enlarge pattern 110%

Make at least 5 copies
of the Bull Moose pattern.

Legend	
←→	**Grain direction**
D	**Dark shade of wood**
MD	**Medium dark shade of wood**
M	**Medium shade of wood**
ML	**Medium light shade of wood**
W	**White pine, aspen, or any white wood**

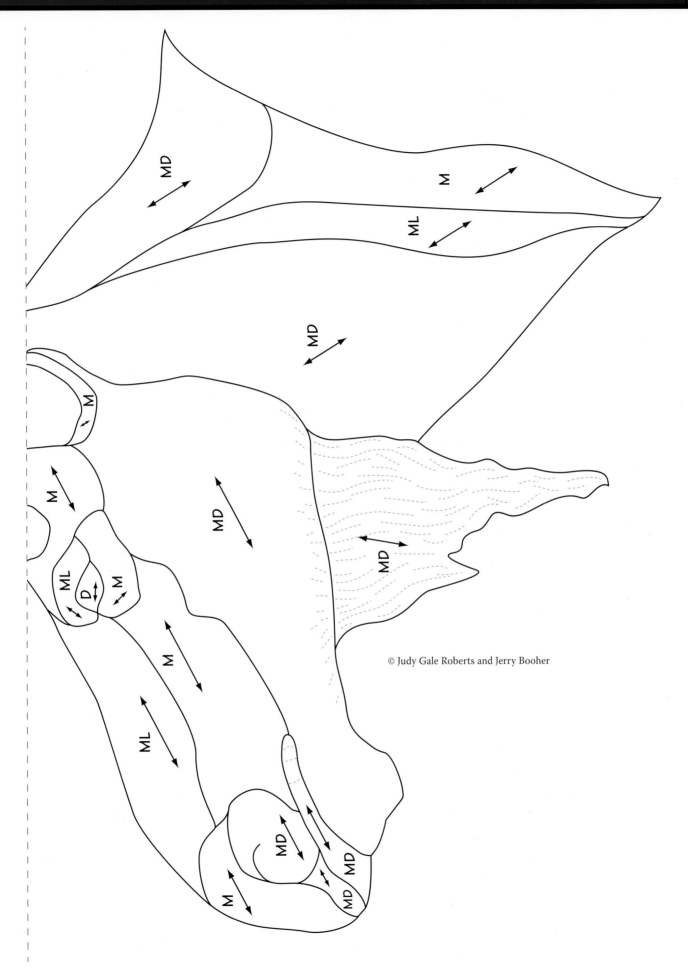

© Judy Gale Roberts and Jerry Booher

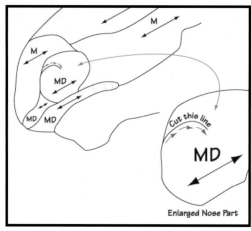

Photo 4.1. The nostril/nose area has a veinlike line. This line should be cut when you are sawing the parts.

Photo 4.2. Cut sanding shims for the head, the neck, and the ear.

Pattern preparation and layout

Step 1 Glance over the pattern. If any areas have color and grain direction that are the same, these areas can be laid out as one section, and then parted later on. Six copies should be enough to complete this project.

Step 2 Divide the pattern accordingly and glue the pieces of the pattern to the wood using a temporary adhesive.

Step 3 Before you cut the parts, notice that the nostril/nose area has a veinlike line. This line should be cut when you are sawing the parts out and will help to define the nostril area. Anytime there is a solid line, like this one, it is intended to be a saw cut line (see **Photo 4.1**).

Checking for fit

Step 4 After you have finished sawing and before you remove the paper, transfer the numbers from the pattern onto the backsides of the parts. When you are satisfied with the fit, remove the paper. At this stage, take a minute to study the project again to get a general idea of what you plan on doing.

Sanding and shaping

Step 5 Make any sanding shims that you are going to need. The Bull Moose's head and neck can be sanded using sanding shims similar to those used on the Wild Mustang (see **Photo 4.2**). Trace around the parts to make the patterns for your sanding shims.

Step 6 Cut out the shims and use double-sided tape to stick the parts together on the ¼" plywood sanding shim.

Step 7 Start with the parts that are in the background, or the parts that are the farthest from the viewer. The back ear is the farthest from the viewer, so this part will be the thinnest. If you do not take much off the surface of this part, you will not be able to take much off the background antler, which will affect all of the parts. Mark a ¼" line around the sides of the part to give yourself a line to sand down to. Then, sand the back ear down to around ¼". Put the part back in place and mark where it joins the back antler, the neck, and the ear in the foreground.

Step 8 Sand the antler in the background. This part needs to be a little thicker than the ear that was just sanded. Sand the back antler down to around ⅜" thick. Make a mark where the back antler joins the foreground antler and any other parts (see **Photo 4.3**). These pencil lines are important guides that will keep you from sanding away too much material.

Step 9 Prepare to sand the head and the neck of the Bull Moose. Turn all the face parts—excluding the eye parts, foreground antler, and the parts just sanded—upside down. Dust off the parts and the backing before putting any tape on. Check to make sure that the sanding shim is flat; any warped pieces will make it almost impossible to keep your parts taped to the shim. Place the double-sided carpet tape on the pieces rather than on the sanding shims (see **Photo 4.4**). Use at least two pieces of tape on each part to hold it down to the shim.

Step 10 Do the same thing for the neck parts. When you are working with two sections like this, it is easier to mark heights with a pencil if you can put the head next to the neck (see **Photo 4.5**).

Photo 4.3. Lower/sand down the back ear and antler.

Photo 4.4. Put double-sided carpet tape on the backs of the parts.

Photo 4.5. Line up the shims to enable you to sand the sections side by side.

Photo 4.6. The parts are taped to the sanding shims.

Photo 4.7. The neck is tapered down toward the head.

Photo 4.8. Sand the beard section, and then mark where it joins the head.

Step 11 When all of the parts are secure, you are ready to start sanding the neck, the beard, and the head (see **Photo 4.6**). The neck has areas that are behind parts of the head, so we will sand the neck first. Remember, we are starting with the thinnest parts and working our way up to the thickest parts. The last part to sand will be a complete part (no parts cutting across it), like the antler on this Bull Moose.

Step 12 Taper the neck down toward the head to about ⅜"; then, round the lower portion of the neck all the way down to the outside edge. On the upper side of the neck, round the neck to the outside edge. Stay above the line showing the thickness of the ear part. If you sand below the pencil line, you run the risk of sanding the ear part a little thinner.

Step 13 Place the neck section next to the head section. Mark the thickness of the just-sanded neck part with a pencil. Get a piece of scrap ¼" plywood to raise the beardlike part to the same height as the other sections on the sanding shims (see **Photo 4.7**). Make a mark where the neck joins the beard.

Step 14 Sand the beard next, staying above the pencil line that shows the thickness of the neck. The beard is in front of the neck, so it will be a little thicker. Taper it down toward the nose section. It needs to stay thicker where it joins the neck, but lower under the face. After shaping the beard, put it back in place and mark where it joins the head (see **Photo 4.8**).

Step 15 Rough in the head. The eye area will be the thickest part of the head, much like the Wild Mustang project. All of the wood will be sanded lower than the eye area. At this point, it would be great for you to have pictures of moose to look at.

Step 16 Taper the head down toward the nose to about ⅜". Then, taper from the eye down to the pencil line indicating the thickness of the neck (see **Photo 4.9**).

Step 17 Work from the eye to the underside of the head. Leaving the eye alone, sand from the eye down to the pencil line indicating the thickness of the beard section. Stay above this line about ⅟₁₆".

Step 18 Go from the eye to the forehead part, tapering back from the upper eyelid part down toward the outer edge. Then, start just below the eye area and round the outside edge down to the nose area. The head is roughed in at this point (see **Photo 4.10**).

Step 19 Rough in the ear. Put it in place and mark where it joins the neck and head sections (see **Photo 4.11**).

Step 20 Taper the ear down to where it joins the head above the jaw line. The ear should look like it attaches to the head and flares out toward the top of the ear. The ear is behind the antler in the foreground, so that end will need to be sanded down at least ⅛" to make it look as though the antler is in front of the ear. Mark ⅛" down on the upper side of the ear to give yourself a target line. First, taper the ear toward the head; then sand it down ⅛" where it meets the antler.

Step 21 Round the backside of the ear, staying above the pencil lines (see **Photo 4.12**). The Bull Moose is almost roughed in at this point (see **Photo 4.13**).

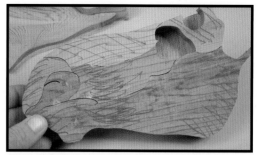

Photo 4.9. Mark on the face of the wood where you plan to sand.

Photo 4.10. The top view shows the angles. The head is roughed in now.

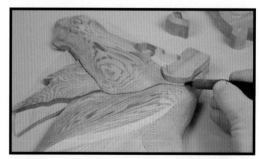

Photo 4.11. Put the ear in place and mark the edge with a pencil.

Photo 4.12. Round the backside of the ear.

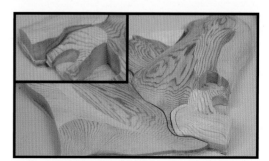

Photo 4.13. Stay above all the pencil lines. The backside is rounded; the front side is thicker.

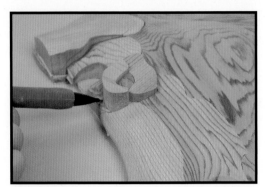

Photo 4.14. Put the eye parts in and mark the sides with your pencil.

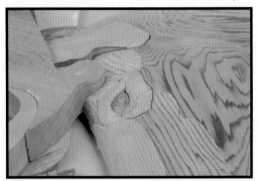

Photo 4.15. Put the foreground antler in place. Put a ¼" shim under it.

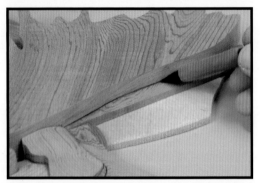

Photo 4.16. Mark any parts that join the antler. Be sure to raise all parts ¼".

Photo 4.17. Note how much material was removed on the forehead.

Step 22 Put the eye parts back in place and mark where the head and the eye parts join (see **Photo 4.14**). You need to stay above these pencil lines as you sand.

Step 23 Start with the lower eye section, tapering it down to match the cheek area and leaving it slightly thicker around the actual eye part. Then, sand the upper eyelid part, doing the same thing. Leave some height along the top edge. Sand the top edge around $\frac{3}{16}$" above the pencil line and taper it toward the eye.

Step 24 Mark the eyeball. Sand it down to the pencil line, then round it slightly to make a dome shape.

Step 25 The antler in the foreground is the last part to rough in. Because the project is temporarily raised ¼" due to the sanding shims, the antler needs to be raised ¼" to match up. Leave the parts on the sanding shim until everything is roughed in. If you accidentally sand too much off the antler, you can easily adjust the head to match. Put the antler in place, using some scrap plywood to raise it up. Mark where the head joins the antler (see **Photo 4.15**).

Step 26 Mark along all of the edges that join the antler, making sure to raise the antler in the background along with the ear to get the right height (see **Photo 4.16**). When you sand the foreground antler, stay above all of these pencil lines. Note how much wood was removed from the forehead section of the Bull Moose (see **Photo 4.17**).

Step 27 Sand the antler part that goes into the head almost down to the pencil line. You are trying to make it look like the antler goes into his head then flares out toward the viewer. Notice the shape of the ear and around the eye area.

Step 28 After you taper the antler toward the head, round the bottom edge down, slightly above the pencil line. Keep this antler thicker than the darker one in the background. After you get the foreground antler roughed in, put all of the parts back together, including the left side of the antler that looks as though it is flipping in the other direction.

Step 29 Raise this antler section using a ¼" scrap piece of plywood. Mark where the two antler parts join to give yourself a line to sand down to (see **Photo 4.18**). Before sanding this section, sand down the little antler prong in the background to at least half the thickness. After sanding this part, put it back in place and mark where it joins the antler (see **Photo 4.19**).

Step 30 Sand the "flip" side of the antler to match where it joins the larger antler part. It can be slightly lower or match exactly. Stay above the line showing the thickness of the little antler prong (see **Photo 4.20**).

Step 31 Round all of the edges along the top portion of the antlers (see **Photo 4.21**). If you have a very small drum sander, you may be able to get into some of these areas. A file or a soft sander, like a hand-held flat or bow sander, can round these areas.

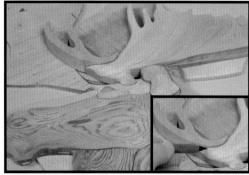

Photo 4.18. Rough in the antler, staying above all pencil marks.

Photo 4.19. Sand the little antler prong in the background, and then mark the side of the antler.

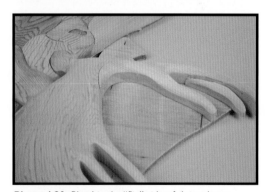

Photo 4.20. Blend in the "flip" side of the antler to match the larger antler section.

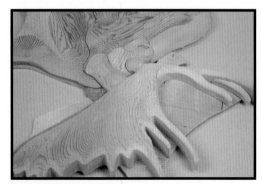

Photo 4.21. The antler is roughed in. Now soften the edges.

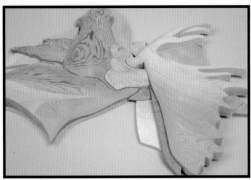

Photo 4.22. The side view of the antler shows it roughed in.

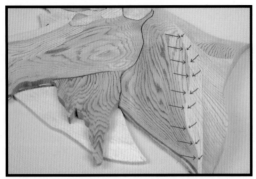

Photo 4.23. Mark the parts to sand to a taper.

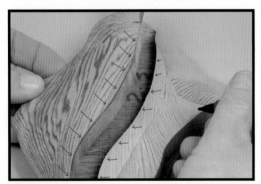

Photo 4.24. Mark ¹⁄₁₆" to ¹⁄₈" down the inside edge. Taper down to this line.

Photo 4.25. Taper the lighter strip part down to the pencil line.

Step 32 Now that all of the parts are roughed in and you are satisfied with the overall dimension of the Bull Moose, you can start cleaning up the parts as you go (see **Photo 4.22**). Check each part and sand any rough marks or cross-grain scratches out of the wood. We use the drum sander wherever possible, then sand by hand.

Step 33 There are some more details following that you can choose to add to the Bull Moose. Check the parts you are working on and clean them as you go. To begin, start taking the parts off the sanding shims.

Step 34 The neck can use some extra contouring. The lighter strip is where the shoulder starts. It is lighter to make it look even more dimensional, and, with a little sanding, the shoulder will stand out. First, taper the neck toward the lighter strip, and then taper the lighter strip down toward the just-sanded neck section (see **Photo 4.23**).

Step 35 Take the larger neck section off the sanding shim, leaving the other three parts on the shim. Mark a line on the inside edge around ¹⁄₁₆" to ¹⁄₈" down (see **Photo 4.24**). Taper the larger neck section down to this pencil line. Sand a gradual taper rather than an abrupt angle down to the line.

Step 36 After sanding the neck section, mark where it joins the lighter strip. Taper the lighter strip down to the pencil line (see **Photo 4.25**). This taper can start on the edge of the lighter strip. When the parts match up, you can sand the three parts still remaining on the sanding shim.

Step 37 Check for any deep scratches, and hand sand where needed. Take all of the parts off the neck sanding shim and work on the head section. Sand the surface of the parts still taped to the sanding shim.

Step 38 Take all of the parts of the face off the sanding shim. Reassemble the entire project, working your way up from the mouth section toward the eye.

Step 39 Take the mouth/lip part out and mark it about ¹⁄₁₆" down. Round down to this pencil line (see **Photo 4.26**).

Step 40 Put the mouth/lip part back in place and mark around it. Lower all of the parts surrounding the mouth/lip part, which means take material off the top/face of the wood to make it thinner. On the lower chin part, take the ¹⁄₁₆" off the whole area below the mouth/lip. On the top side, you can taper from the nostril down to the pencil line (see **Photo 4.27**).

Step 41 The nostril can use some more definition. The vein-like saw cut that was made will help add detail for the nostril. Carve or burn to darken the nostril. We carved and used the woodburner to add the nostril. A round-edged X-acto knife will do any light carving on intarsia projects. Mark the area first (see **Photo 4.28**); then carve toward the saw cut line on the lower side of the saw cut line.

Step 42 Hand sand the carved area to make the area look softer (see **Photo 4.29**). Then, use the woodburner to darken the actual nostril after the Bull Moose is roughed in.

Photo 4.26. Mark ¹⁄₁₆" down around the mouth/lip part. Round the sides down to this line.

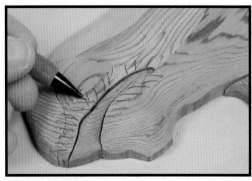

Photo 4.27. After sanding the mouth/lip part, put it back in place and mark the adjoining parts. Taper the nose area down toward the pencil line indicating the thickness of the mouth. Lower/sand down the chin area below the pencil line.

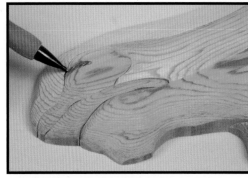

Photo 4.28. Carve the nostril to give more definition.

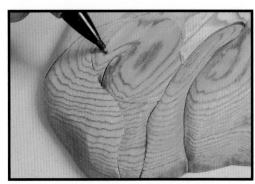

Photo 4.29. After carving, sand the nostril smooth.

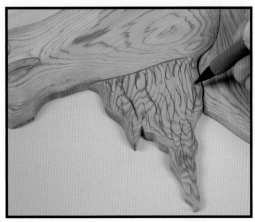

Photo 4.30. Mark lines to follow for adding texture.

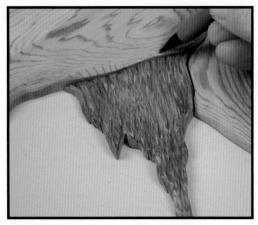

Photo 4.31. Extend the lines onto the lower jaw to blend in.

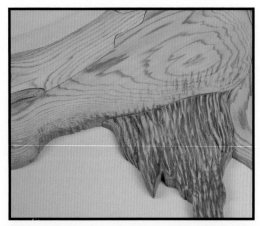

Photo 4.32. Texture is added to the lower jaw to blend the beard.

Step 43 To make the beard part look more like strands of fur, add some hairlike texture to the surface. First, mark some guidelines to follow as you carve in these lines with the Wonder Wheel (see **Photo 4.30**). Use the dashed lines on the pattern as a guide. (For more information on using the Wonder Wheel, see the "Adding Texture" section on page 11.) If you do not have a Wonder Wheel, you can carve these lines in.

Step 44 Put the beard part back in place and mark some lines extending up from the beard onto the lower face (see **Photo 4.31** and **4.32**). This will help to make a gradual blend from the untextured to the textured area. The texture will not have as much contrast when you apply the finish.

Step 45 Burnish the eye using the edge of the Wonder Wheel. It will darken the eye and give it a sheen to make it stand out more (see **Photo 4.33**). You could also use a woodburner to darken the eye. To add the highlight, use a small dowel made out of aspen (see **Photo 4.34**).

Hand sand each part

Step 46 Go over each part. Hold it up to the light to see if there are any humps, bumps, or scratches. When you hold the part up to the light, it will help you to spot areas that need more work.

Step 47 Hand sand the edges, barely knocking off the sharp corners on all parts. Erase any pencil lines that may be showing. Check again for any deep scratches (see **Photo 4.35**).

Applying the finish

Step 48 Dust or blow off all of the parts. Finish the Bull Moose by referring back to the instructions for finishing the Bald Eagle in Chapter Two, page 30, and the "Applying the finish" section in Chapter One on page 13.

Make the backing

Step 49 After the finish has dried, create a backing for the piece from ¼" luan plywood. Refer to the instructions for making a backing in Chapter Two, page 30, and in Chapter One, page 14.

Glue the Bull Moose down

Step 50 Use the beard, the larger antler, and the *MD* upper back of the neck parts to lock in the project using the combination of yellow wood glue and hot melt glue. Once these parts are in place, use dots of the yellow wood glue to hold the rest of the parts in place. Allow the glue to set before putting on the hanger.

Put on the hanger

Step 51 Hang the project by installing a mirror hanger. Refer to the "Installing the Hanger" section in Chapter One on page 15 for more instructions. Clean up the tail part, sanding any exposed areas.

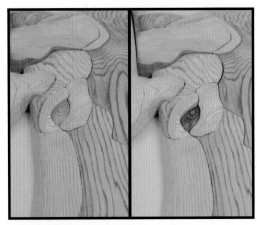

Photo 4.33. You can burnish the eye with a Wonder Wheel.

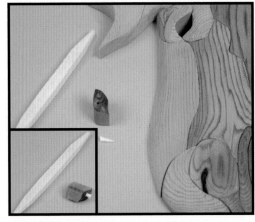

Photo 4.34. Aspen cut to fit in a pencil sharpener is used to create the dowel for the eye highlight.

Photo 4.35. Check for any imperfections and hand sand the parts as necessary. Erase any pencil lines and knock any sharp corners off most parts. The Bull Moose is now ready for finishing.

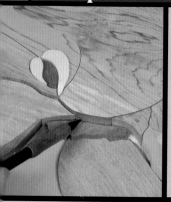

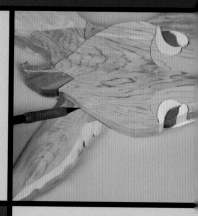

Wild Burro Project

Wood

- ■ Dark shade of wood at least 5" wide by 5" long and ¾" thick
- ■ Medium-dark shade of wood at least 3" wide by 4 ½" long and ¾" thick
- ■ Medium shade of wood at least 5" wide by 24" long and ¾" thick
- ■ Medium-light shade of wood at least 4" wide by 5" long and ¾" thick
- ■ Light shade of wood at least 5" wide by 10" long and ¾" thick
- ■ White shade of wood at least 3" wide by 5" long and ¾" thick
- ■ ¼" luan plywood for the backing and sanding shim

Note: As you progress through the patterns in this book, there will be less and less instruction. It is good to start relying on the experience you have to guide you through shaping these projects. We will mention some things to look out for and give some recommendations on the following projects.

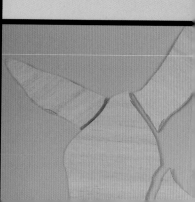

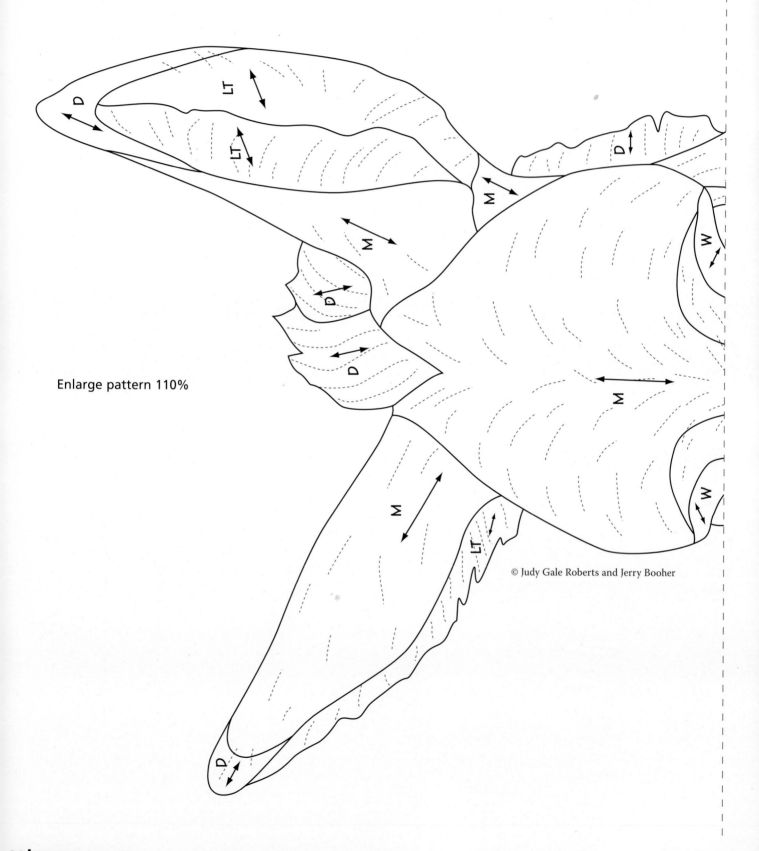

Enlarge pattern 110%

© Judy Gale Roberts and Jerry Booher

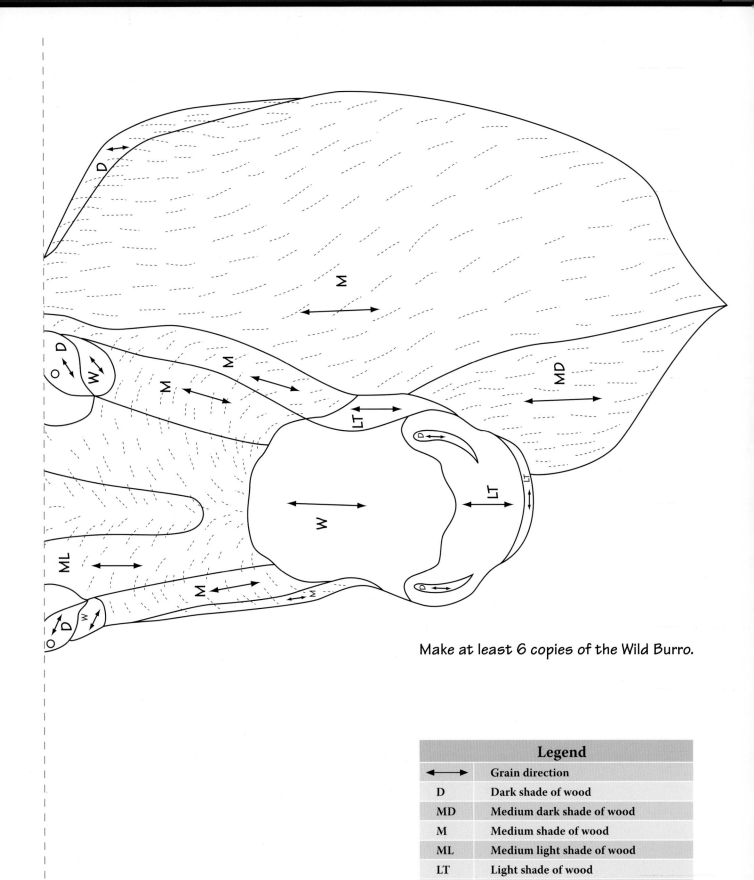

Make at least 6 copies of the Wild Burro.

Legend	
←→	Grain direction
D	Dark shade of wood
MD	Medium dark shade of wood
M	Medium shade of wood
ML	Medium light shade of wood
LT	Light shade of wood
W	White pine, aspen, or any white wood

Photo 5.1. Make a sanding shim for the head, the ears, and the neck.

Photo 5.2. Sand the mane first, and then mark where it joins the rest of the parts.

Pattern preparation and layout

Step 1 Study the pattern. Lay out any areas with the same color and grain direction as one section. Six copies should be enough to complete this project. Label one of the pattern copies as your master.

Step 2 Get your wood as dust free as possible, and then glue the patterns to the wood. Mark arrows on all of the outside edges.

Checking for fit

Step 3 Once all of the pieces have been cut and before you remove the paper, transfer the numbers from the pattern to the backsides of the parts. Assemble the project. When you are satisfied with the fit, remove the paper. Study the project again to form a general shaping plan.

Sanding and shaping

Step 4 Make any sanding shims that you will need for the project. The Wild Burro's head, ears, and neck can be sanded using sanding shims similar to those used on the previous patterns (see **Photo 5.1**). Trace around the parts to make the patterns for your sanding shims. Then, cut the shims from ¼" plywood.

Step 5 The mane would be the farthest from the viewer, so sand it first. It is easier to sand this part before taping all of the parts to the sanding shims. After sanding the mane, mark where it joins the neck, the head, and the ear (see **Photo 5.2**).

Step 6 Use double-sided tape to adhere all of the parts to the sanding shims (including the ears, the head, and the neck). Remember that the parts taped to the shims will be ¼" thicker while you are working with the shim. Have some scrap plywood handy to check the thicknesses of the parts that are next to the sections taped onto sanding shims to compensate for height differences between the parts on sanding shims and the parts not on shims.

Step 7 Taper the left ear down toward the head. We sanded ours down to around ¼" where it meets the head. Round the backside of the ear and leave the underside thicker.

Step 8 Put the left ear back in place and mark where it joins the head (see **Photo 5.3**). Then, sand the ear on the right. Since the mane on top starts out in front of the head and then goes back behind the right ear, leave some material on the right ear where it joins the mane. This is an area you will have to slowly match up.

Step 9 Taper the right ear down toward the head. Sand it down to around ½" thick where it joins the head. Round the *M* part of the right ear down to about half the thickness of the wood. Leave the outer side thicker (the part next to the two *LT* pieces).

Step 10 Rough in the neck section, tapering it down toward the face. We sanded the neck down to around ⅜" where it joins the head (see **Photo 5.4**). The outside edges will be thicker. Watch the line indicating the thickness of the mane; stay above it.

Step 11 Rough in the head, staying above all of the lines around the head. Once all of the parts are close to the thicknesses desired, you can start taking the parts off the sanding shims.

Step 12 Detail the eyes by lowering the parts above and below the white sections around the eyes. Then, taper the white parts down to meet the parts you just sanded. Round the eyes.

Step 13 Lower the nostrils at least ⅛". Sand the lower lip down below the upper lip. Stay above the *MD* neck part below the mouth.

Step 14 Put the mane section between the ears in place and mark where it joins the rest of the head. The front portion of the mane will be thicker than the head; sand the portion behind the ear thinner. Give the ear some depth by sanding the outer *LT* section down toward the inside edge.

Step 15 Put the highlight in the eyes using the same technique shown on page 29 in the Bald Eagle Demonstration.

Step 16 A burro's coat is shaggy, so use the Wonder Wheel to add some texture. Follow the dashed lines on the pattern. Use a lighter/finer texture starting from the nose up. Carve deeper grooves on the mane and on the ears (see **Photo 5.5**).

Step 17 Apply the finish on the Wild Burro, and then make your backing. Refer to the Bald Eagle Demonstration, pages 30 to 31, and to pages 13 to 15 in Chapter One for specific instructions on applying the finish and making a backing.

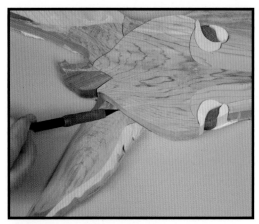

Photo 5.3. Sand the left ear next. Mark where it joins the head.

Photo 5.4. Taper the neck toward the head, and then rough in the head. Use some scrap plywood to raise the mane to the same thickness as the parts on the sanding shims.

Photo 5.5. Note the texture, the detail around the eyes, and the insides of the ears. The texture is deeper on the mane and inside the ears. The nostrils have been lowered.

Polar Bear Project

Wood

- Dark shade of wood at least 3" wide by 4" long and ¾" thick
- Medium shade of wood at least 4" wide by 3" long and ¾" thick
- Light shade of wood at least 3" wide by 3" long and ¾" thick.
- White shade of wood at least 9" wide by 24" long and ¾" thick
- ¼" luan plywood for the backing and sanding shim

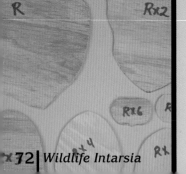

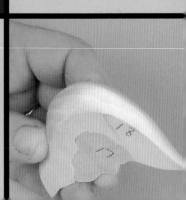

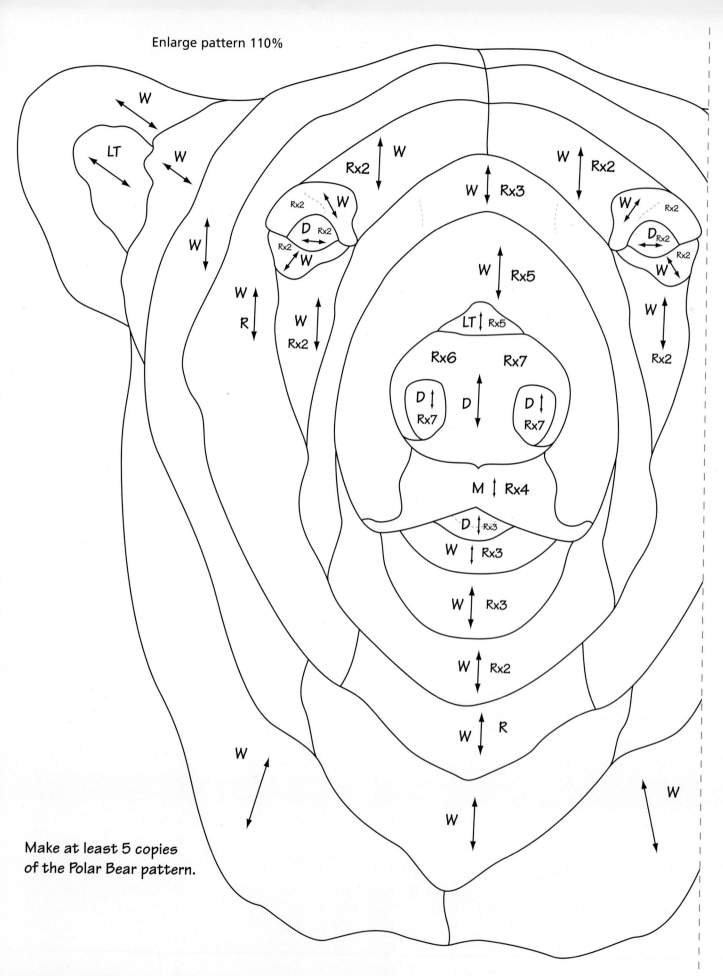

Enlarge pattern 110%

Make at least 5 copies
of the Polar Bear pattern.

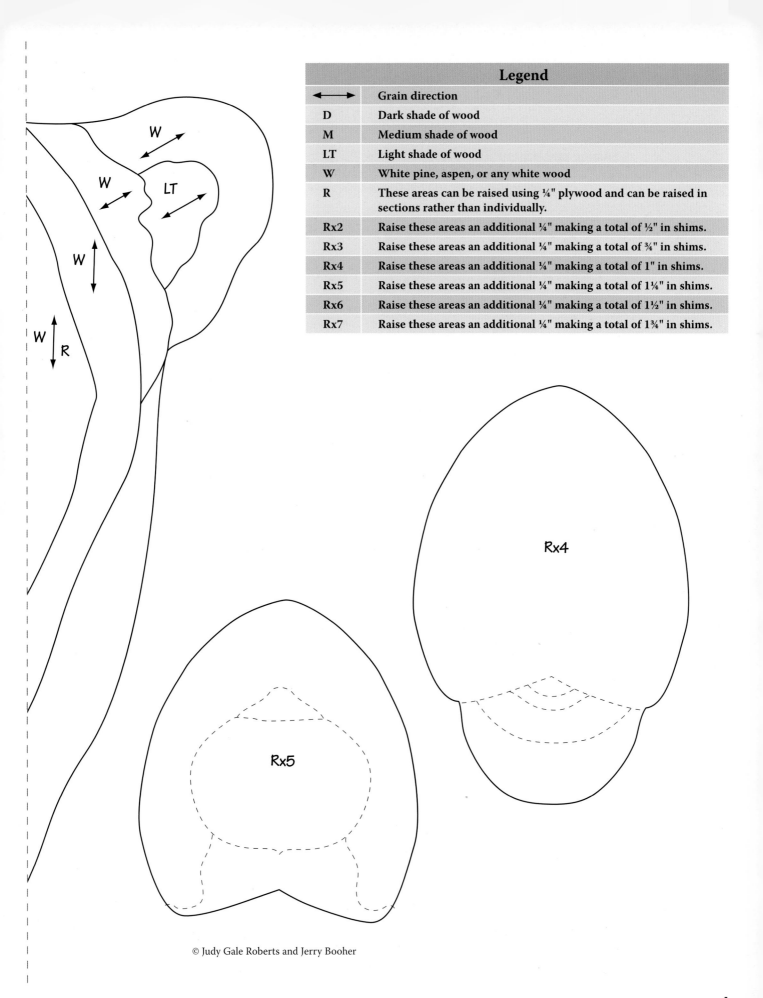

Legend	
↔	Grain direction
D	Dark shade of wood
M	Medium shade of wood
LT	Light shade of wood
W	White pine, aspen, or any white wood
R	These areas can be raised using ¼" plywood and can be raised in sections rather than individually.
Rx2	Raise these areas an additional ¼" making a total of ½" in shims.
Rx3	Raise these areas an additional ¼" making a total of ¾" in shims.
Rx4	Raise these areas an additional ¼" making a total of 1" in shims.
Rx5	Raise these areas an additional ¼" making a total of 1¼" in shims.
Rx6	Raise these areas an additional ¼" making a total of 1½" in shims.
Rx7	Raise these areas an additional ¼" making a total of 1¾" in shims.

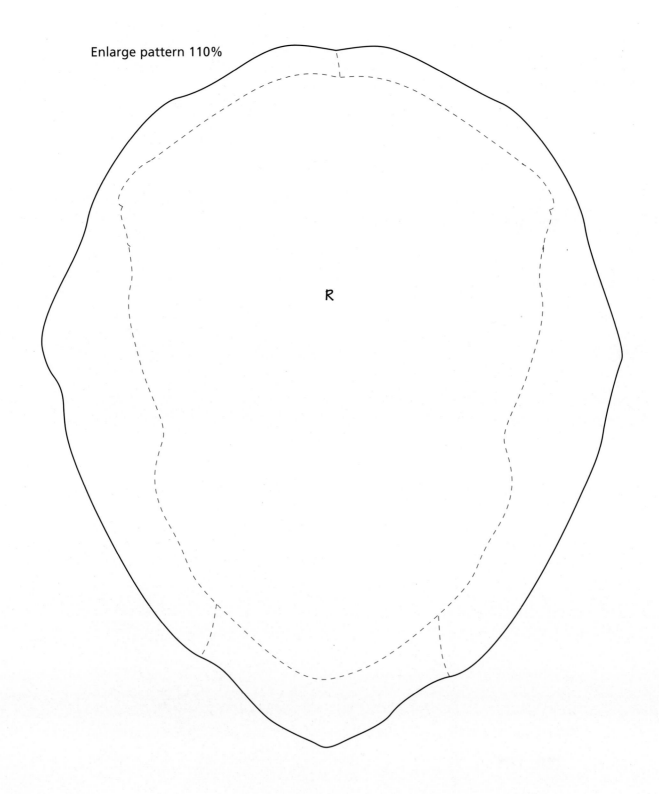

Enlarge pattern 110%

R

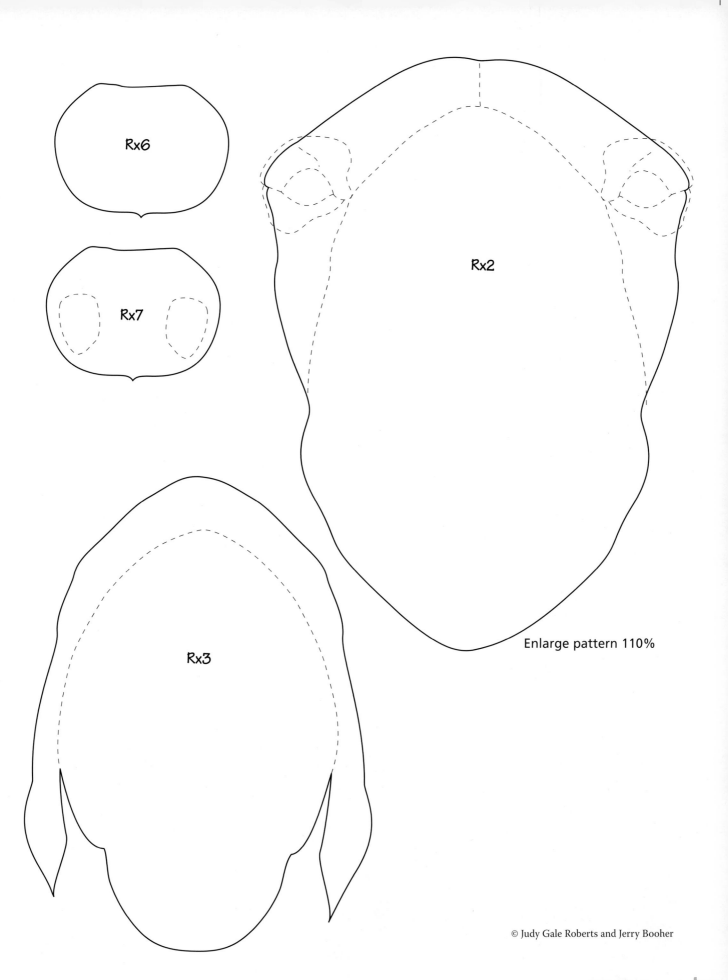

Rx6

Rx7

Rx2

Rx3

Enlarge pattern 110%

© Judy Gale Roberts and Jerry Booher

Photo 6.1. Sanding shims are great for sanding consistent contours on sections like the head and ears.

Sanding and shaping

Step 1 Once all of the pieces have been cut and you have checked the fit, make any sanding shims that you will need for the project. The Polar Bear's head and ears can be sanded using sanding shims similar to those used on previous patterns (see **Photo 6.1**). Trace around the parts to make the patterns for your sanding shims. The Polar Bear also has seven raising shims, which work to "pull" the face out. This can look very dimensional and gives the Polar Bear character. Make sure the plywood you use to create raising and sanding shims is flat (see **Photo 6.2**).

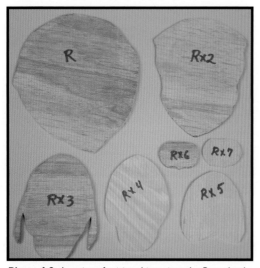

Photo 6.2. A series of raising shims gives the Bear depth.

Photo 6.3. Put the raising shims in place.

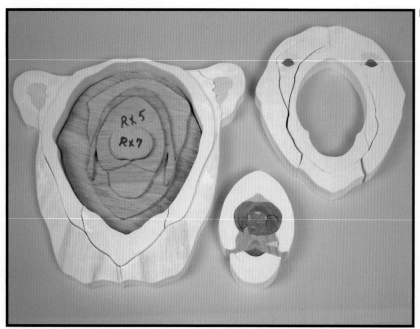

Step 2 Sand the two neck sections first. Mark where these two parts join the rest of the head.

Step 3 Tape all of the parts, putting all the raising shims in place (see **Photo 6.3** and **6.4**). Use double-sided tape to stick the parts together on the ¼" plywood sanding shims. In this case, it will be easier to put the double-sided tape on each shim and then place the parts on top of the shim.

Step 4 Blend in all of the raised areas and smooth out the "stair-step" look made by placing all of the ¼" raising shims under the wood. Sand these areas together as a unit on the sanding shim.

Step 5 Undercut the backside the Polar Bear's ears (see **Photo 6.5**). Relieving the backside can make the project look even more dimensional. Do not make it a very sharp angle; if you do, it will be very hard to trace when you make the backing (see **Photo 6.6**).

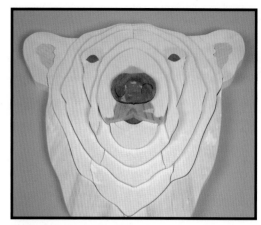

Photo 6.4. Raising shims "pull" the face out for more dimension.

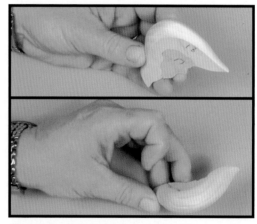

Photo 6.5. Undercutting the backside of the ears will give the Polar Bear even more dimension.

Photo 6.6. The Polar Bear finish sanded. Note the lowered nostrils, the highlights on the eyes, the lowered inside ear parts, the thicker eyelids, and the lower lip that is a little thicker than the chin.

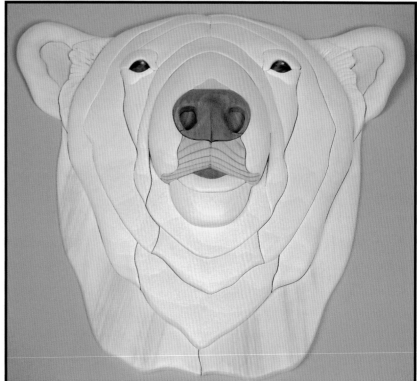

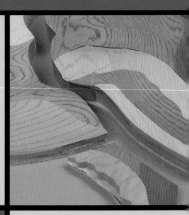

Red Fox Project

Wood

- Dark shade of wood at least 3" wide by 7 ½" long and ¾" thick
- Medium-dark shade of wood at least 2" wide by 2" long and ¾" thick
- Medium shade of wood at least 7 ½" wide by 11" long and ¾" thick
- Medium-light shade of wood at least 6" wide by 10" long and ¾" thick
- Light shade of wood at least 7" wide by 13" long and ¾" thick.
- White shade of wood at least 3 ½" wide by 4" long and ¾" thick
- ¼" luan plywood for the backing and sanding shim

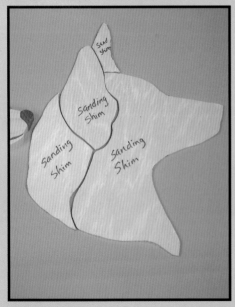

Photo 7.1. Sanding shims are used for shaping the Red Fox.

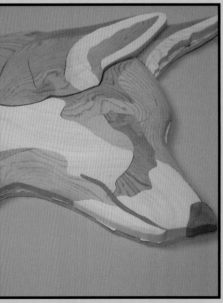

Photo 7.2. Tape the parts to the sanding shims using double-sided carpet tape. Tape the sections so they will line up.

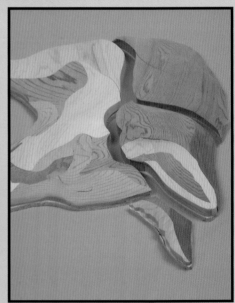

Photo 7.3. Note the sections taped to the sanding shims. Rough in all of the parts while they are taped to the sanding shims. This will give your project a nice, consistent shape.

Enlarge pattern 110%

Make at least 5 copies
of the Red Fox pattern.

Legend	
←——→	**Grain direction**
D	**Dark shade of wood**
MD	**Medium dark shade of wood**
M	**Medium shade of wood**
ML	**Medium light shade of wood**
LT	**Light shade of wood**
W	**White pine, aspen, or any white wood**

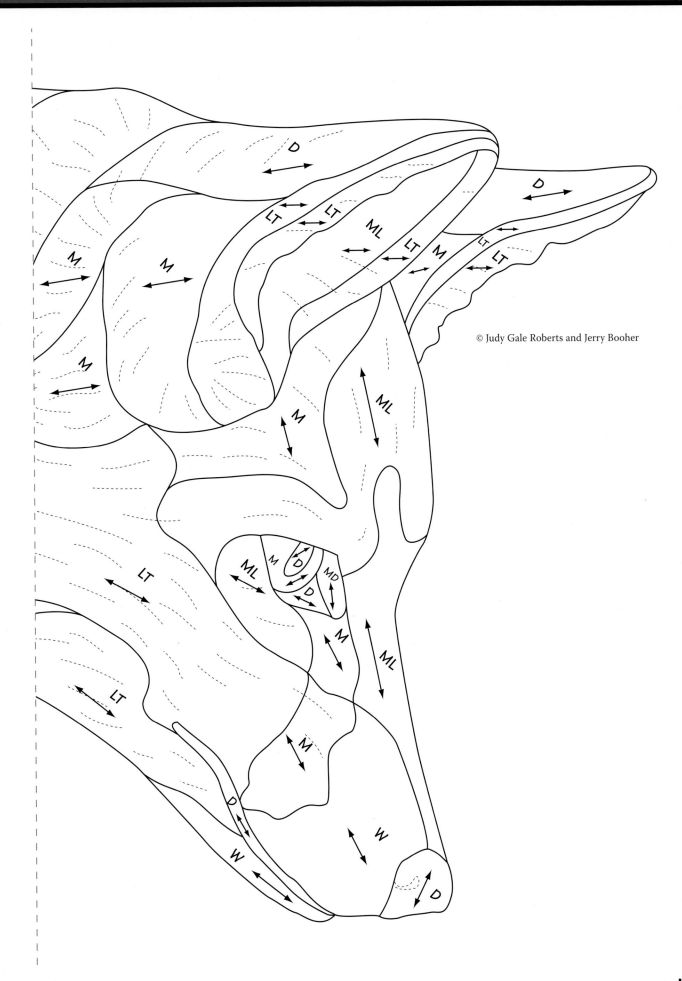

© Judy Gale Roberts and Jerry Booher

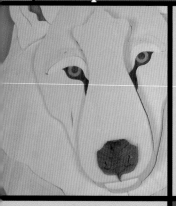

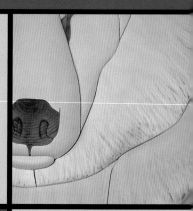

Arctic Wolf Project

Wood

- ☐ Dark shade of wood at least 3" wide by 4" long and ¾" thick
- ☐ Medium shade of wood at least 2 ½" wide by 3 ½" long and ¾" thick
- ☐ White shade of wood at least 9 ½" wide by 28" long and ¾" thick
- ☐ ¼" luan plywood for the backing and sanding shim

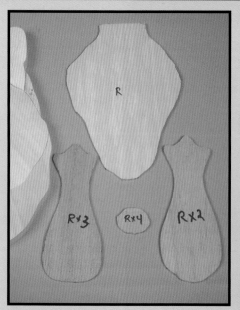

Photo 8.1. Raising shims are used on the Arctic Wolf. Cut the shims smaller than the actual parts to be raised.

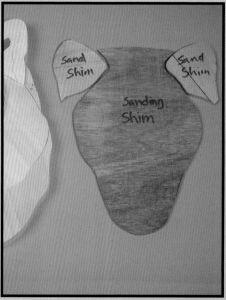

Photo 8.2. Sanding shims are used on the Wolf. Use double-sided carpet tape to hold the wood to the sanding shims. Sand the parts around the face first; then, mark where they join the face. Next, tape the parts with the raising shims to the sanding shims.

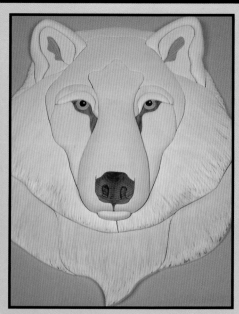

Photo 8.3. The Wolf is finish sanded. Note that some texture was applied to the Wolf's coat. Also, note the highlights added to the eyes, the nostrils that are lowered, and the smooth transition from the forehead to the nose.

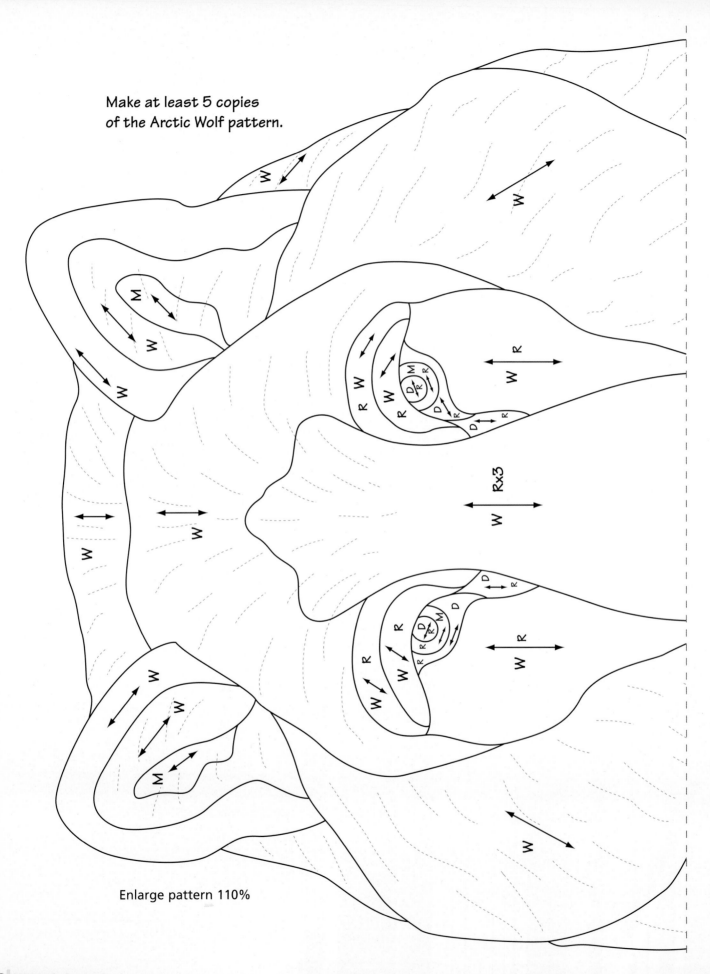

Make at least 5 copies
of the Arctic Wolf pattern.

Enlarge pattern 110%

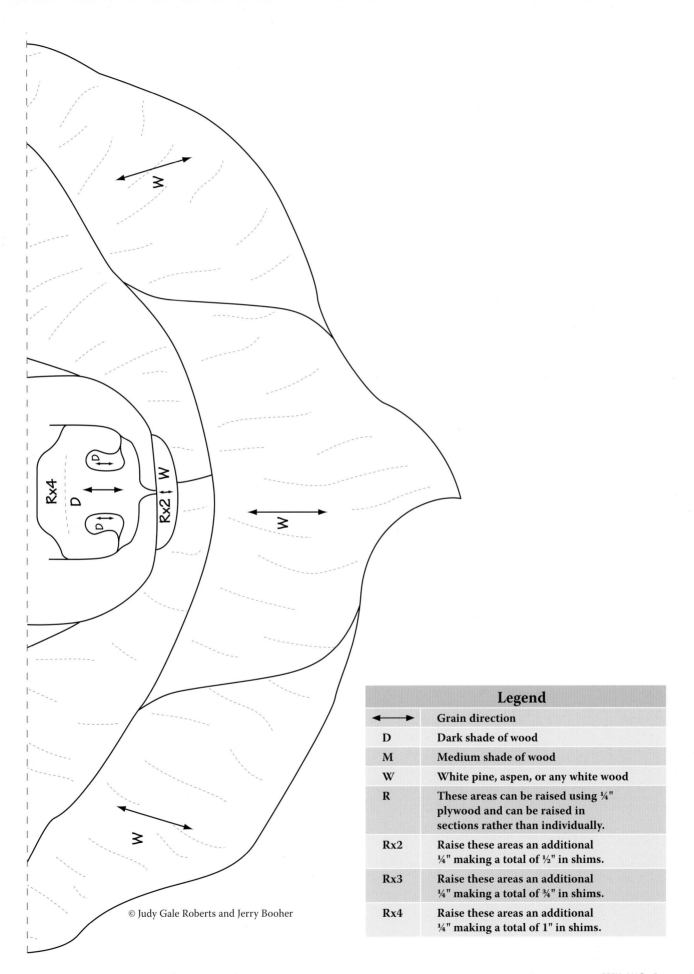

© Judy Gale Roberts and Jerry Booher

Legend	
Grain direction	Grain direction
D	Dark shade of wood
M	Medium shade of wood
W	White pine, aspen, or any white wood
R	These areas can be raised using ¼" plywood and can be raised in sections rather than individually.
Rx2	Raise these areas an additional ¼" making a total of ½" in shims.
Rx3	Raise these areas an additional ¼" making a total of ¾" in shims.
Rx4	Raise these areas an additional ¼" making a total of 1" in shims.

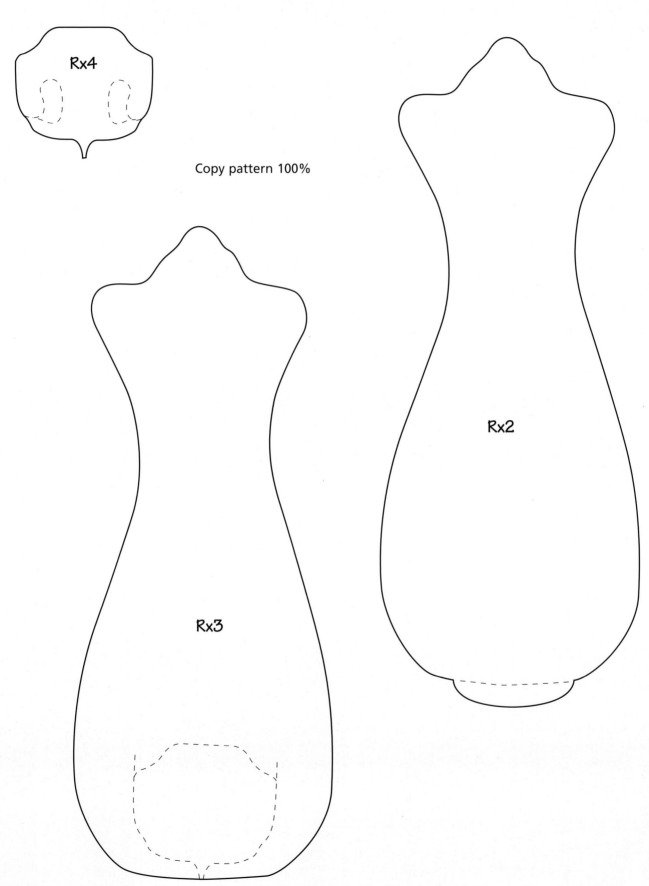

Rx4

Copy pattern 100%

Rx2

Rx3

© Judy Gale Roberts and Jerry Booher

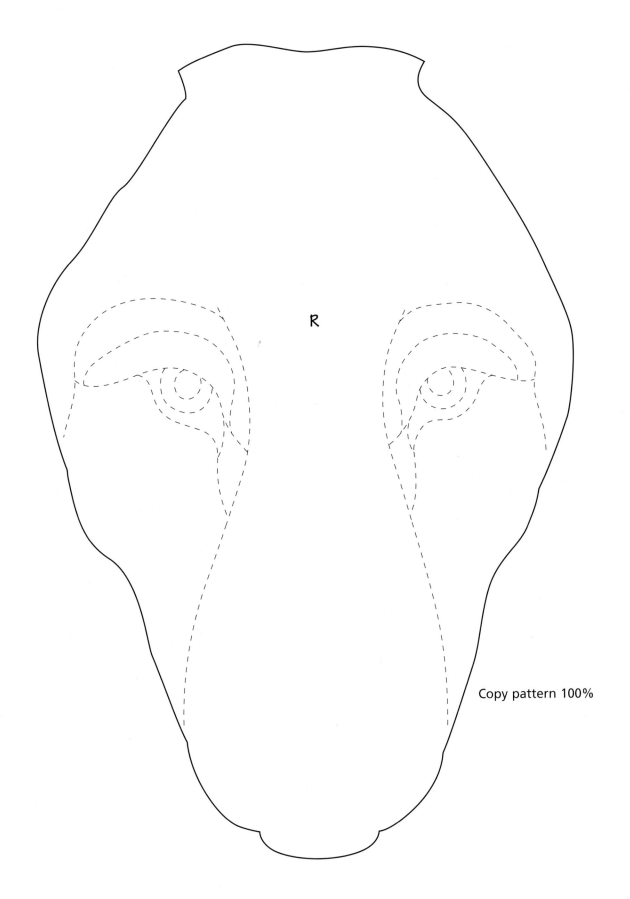

R

Copy pattern 100%

© Judy Gale Roberts and Jerry Booher

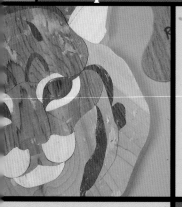

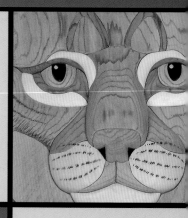

Bobcat Project

Wood

- Dark shade of wood at least 5" wide by 11" long and ¾" thick
- Medium-dark shade of wood at least 6" wide by 7" long and ¾" thick
- Medium shade of wood at least 8" wide by 9" long and ¾" thick
- Medium-light shade of wood at least 7" wide by 17" long and ¾" thick
- White shade of wood at least 5" wide by 12" long and ¾" thick
- ¼" luan plywood for the backing and sanding shim

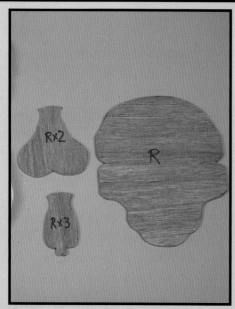

Photo 9.1. Raising shims are used on the Bobcat. Cut the shims smaller than the actual parts to be raised.

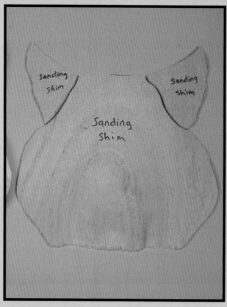

Photo 9.2. Sanding shims are used on the Bobcat. Use double-sided carpet tape to hold the wood to the sanding shims. Tape the raising shims in place as you sand the face.

Photo 9.3. The Bobcat is now finish sanded. Note the texture applied to the Bobcat's coat. The texture is coarser around the outside edges. Also, the highlights are added to the eyes and the nostrils are burned, along with some spots on the cheeks and the muzzle.

Make at least 5 copies
of the Bobcat pattern.

Legend	
⟷	**Grain direction**
D	Dark shade of wood
MD	Medium dark shade of wood
M	Medium shade of wood
ML	Medium light shade of wood
W	White pine, aspen, or any white wood
R	These areas can be raised using ¼" plywood and can be raised in sections rather than individually.
Rx2	Raise these areas an additional ¼" making a total of ½" in shims.
Rx3	Raise these areas an additional ¼" making a total of ¾" in shims.

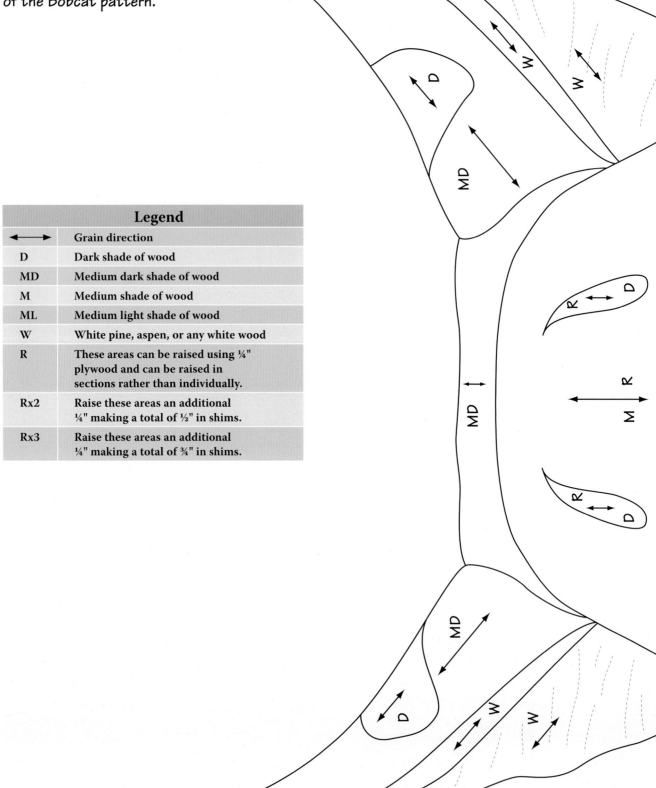

Enlarge pattern 110%

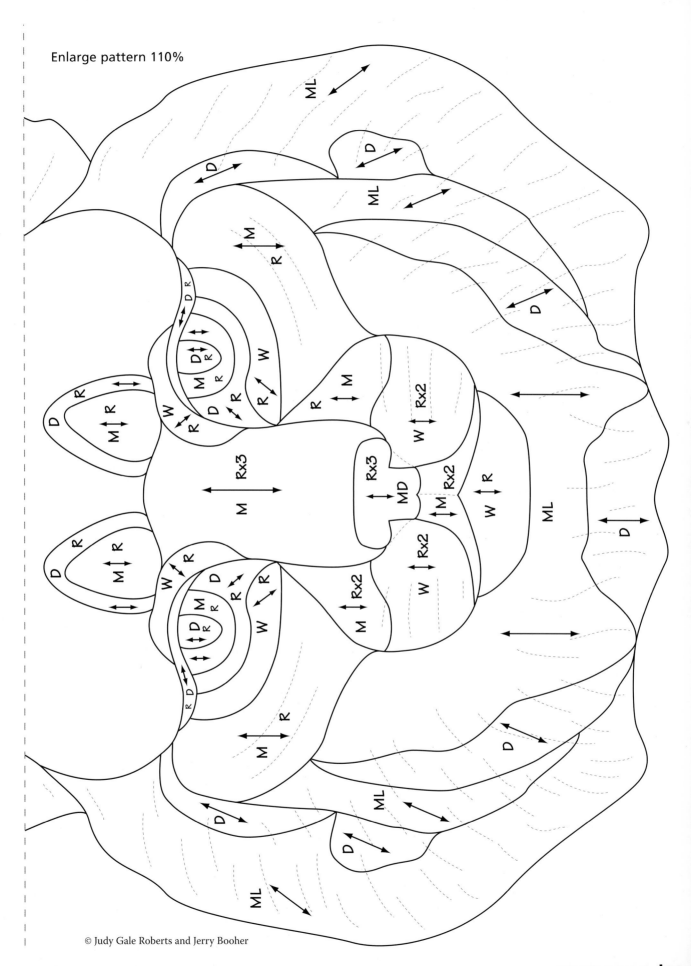

© Judy Gale Roberts and Jerry Booher

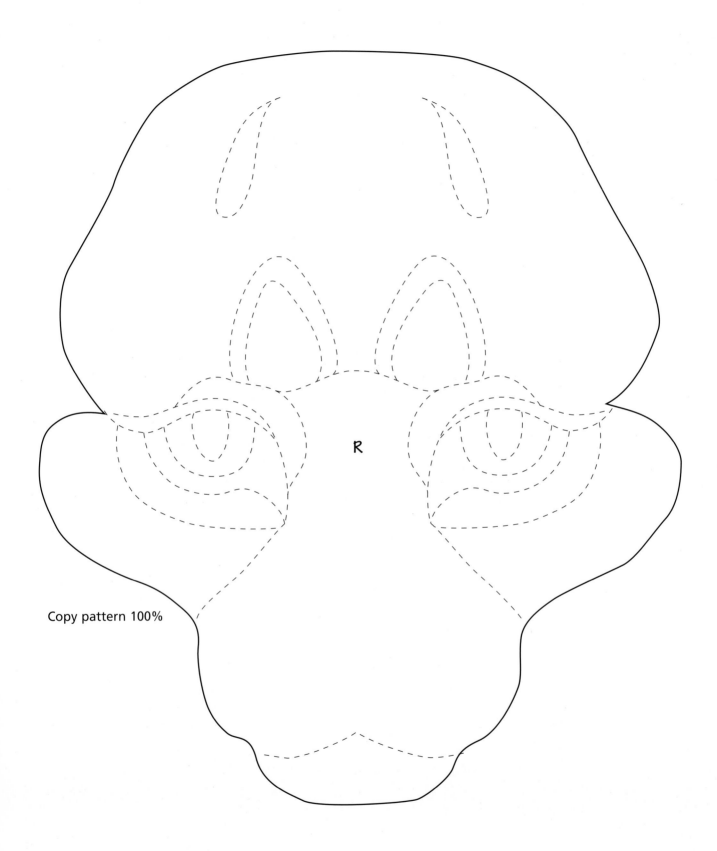

R

Copy pattern 100%

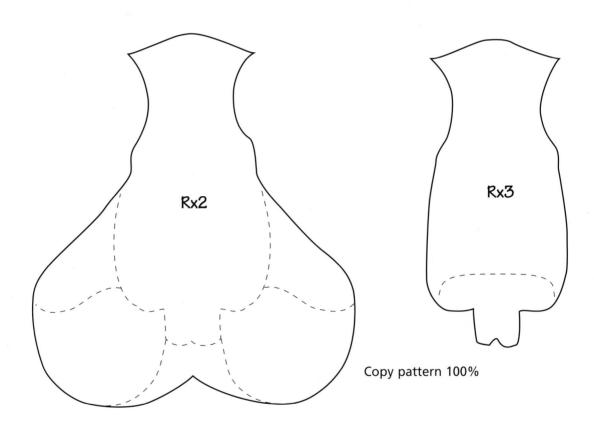

Rx2

Rx3

Copy pattern 100%

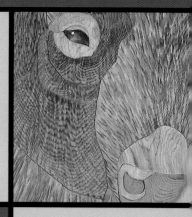

Buffalo Project

Wood

- Dark shade of wood at least 6" wide by 20" long and ¾" thick
- Medium-dark shade of wood at least 8" wide by 19" long and ¾" thick
- ¼" luan plywood for the backing and sanding shim

Photo 10.1. Raising shims and sanding shims are used on the Buffalo. Cut the raising shims smaller than the actual parts to be raised. Use double-sided carpet tape to apply the parts to the sanding shims.

Photo 10.2. The Buffalo is finish sanded. Texture is applied to almost all of the surfaces of the Buffalo's parts (the eye area, the horns, and the nose area have no texture). The texture is coarser around the outside edges. Also, the highlights are added to the eye, the nostrils are lowered, the ear is dished out, and the raised eye-area parts are blended back into the Buffalo's face.

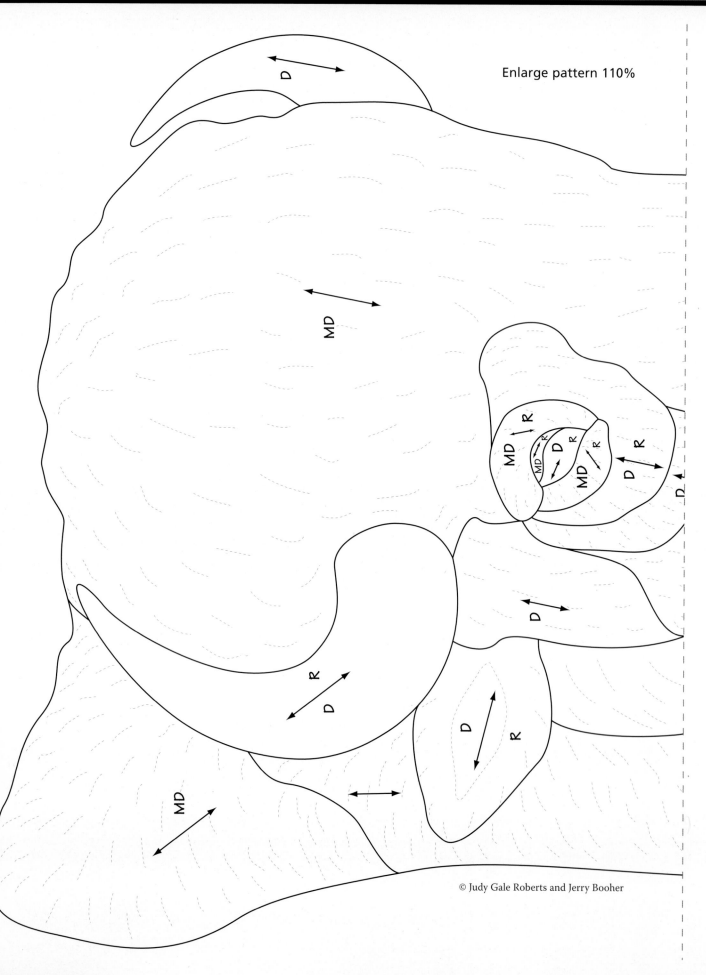

Enlarge pattern 110%

© Judy Gale Roberts and Jerry Booher

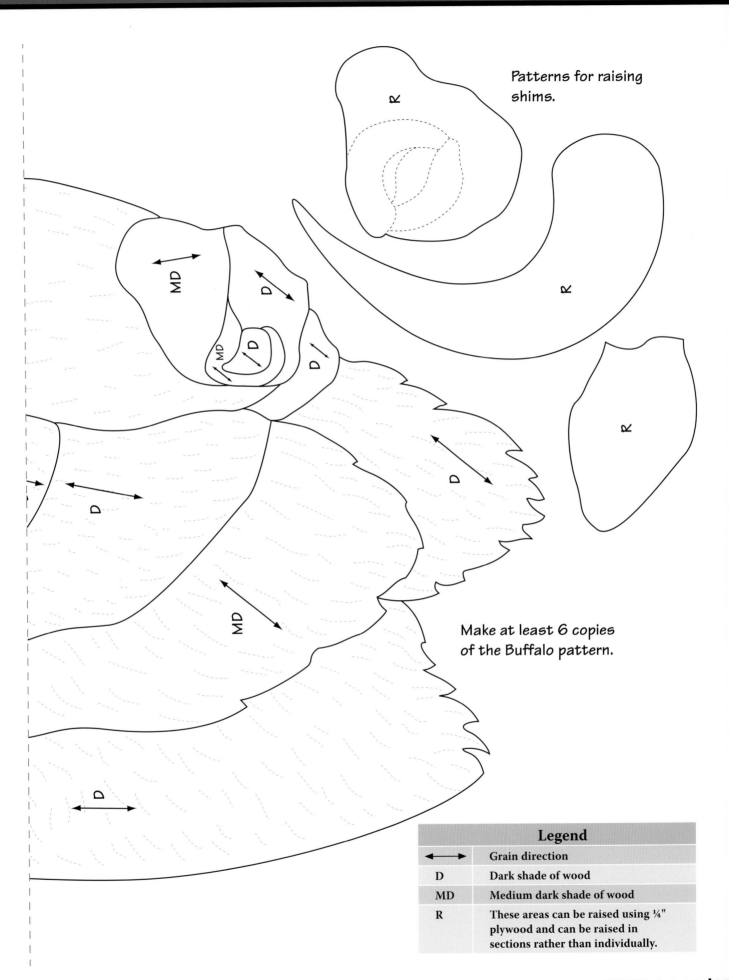

Patterns for raising shims.

Make at least 6 copies of the Buffalo pattern.

Legend	
⟷	**Grain direction**
D	**Dark shade of wood**
MD	**Medium dark shade of wood**
R	**These areas can be raised using ¼" plywood and can be raised in sections rather than individually.**

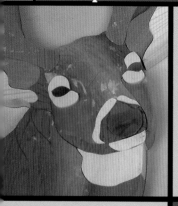

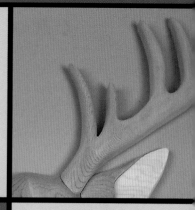

White-Tailed Deer Project

Wood

- Dark shade of wood at least 2" wide by 2 ½" long and ¾" thick
- Medium-dark shade of wood at least 3" wide by 5" long and ¾" thick
- Medium shade of wood at least 6" wide by 14" long and ¾" thick
- Medium-light shade of wood at least 6" wide by 14 ½" long and ¾" thick
- Light shade of wood at least 3 ½" wide by 7" long and ¾" thick.
- White shade of wood at least 3" wide by 6" long and ¾" thick
- ¼" luan plywood for the backing and sanding shim

Photo 11.1. Raising shims and sanding shims are used on the White-Tailed Deer. Use flat plywood for all of the shims. When taping the parts to the sanding shims, be sure to tape the raised nose section in place. Use double-sided carpet tape to apply the parts to the sanding shims.

Photo 11.2. The White-Tailed Deer has been finish sanded. Note that the nostrils are burned in. Also, the highlights are added to the eye, the ears are dished out, and the raised nose area is blended back into the White-Tailed Deer's face. In addition, the edges of the antlers are softened.

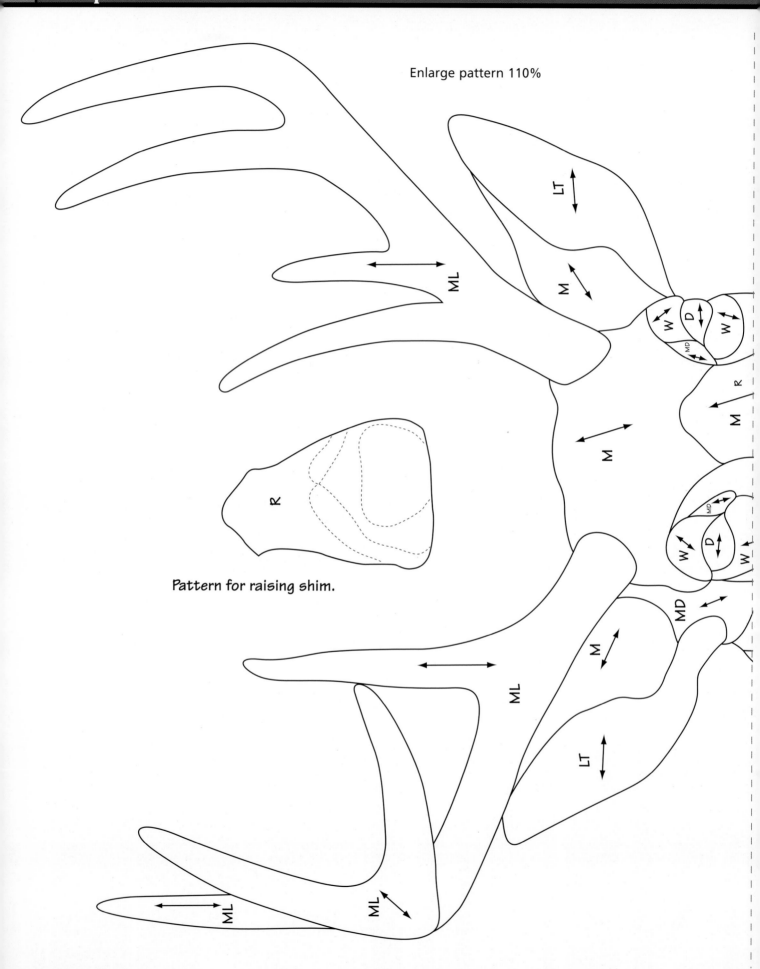

Enlarge pattern 110%

Pattern for raising shim.

Make at least 6 copies
of the White-Tailed Deer pattern.

Legend	
⟷	Grain direction
D	Dark shade of wood
MD	Medium dark shade of wood
M	Medium shade of wood
ML	Medium light shade of wood
LT	Light shade of wood
W	White pine, aspen, or any white wood
R	These areas can be raised using ¼" plywood and can be raised in sections rather than individually.

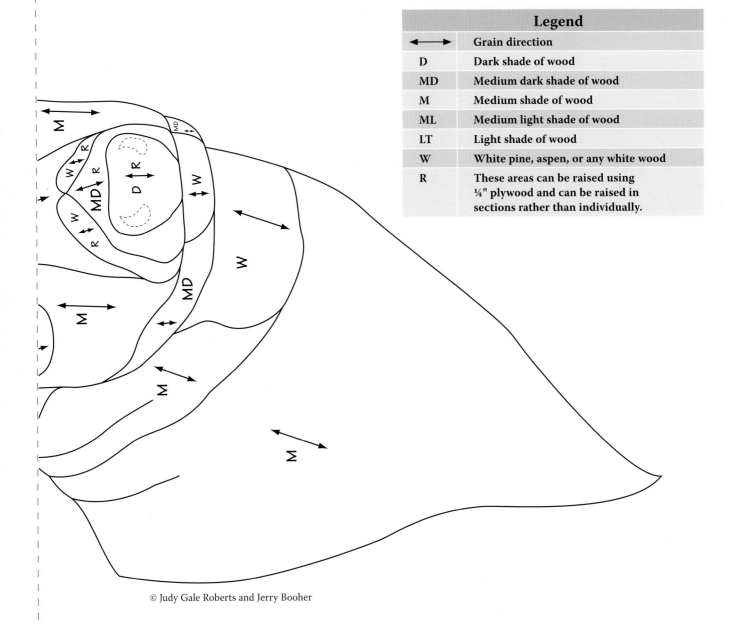

© Judy Gale Roberts and Jerry Booher

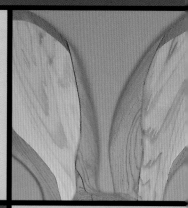

Jack Rabbit Project

Wood

- Dark shade of wood at least 2 ½" wide by 2 ½" long and ¾" thick
- Medium-dark shade of wood at least 4" wide by 14" long and ¾" thick
- Medium shade of wood at least 4" wide by 10" long and ¾" thick
- Medium-light shade of wood at least 6" wide by 16" long and ¾" thick
- Light shade of wood at least 6" wide by 16" long and ¾" thick.
- ¼" luan plywood for the backing and sanding shim

Photo 12.1. Sanding shims are used on the Jack Rabbit. Use double-sided carpet tape to apply the parts to the sanding shims. Leave the eye parts out when you tape the rest of the parts to the sanding shims. The eye will be thicker. After all of the parts are roughed in, put the eye parts in and mark around them. Stay above these lines when sanding the eye.

Photo 12.2. The Jack Rabbit is finish sanded. The nostril is burned in and the pupil was darkened using the woodburner. The whisker detail was added with the woodburner also. Note the highlights added to the eye. The ears are cupped to give them more of a hollow look.

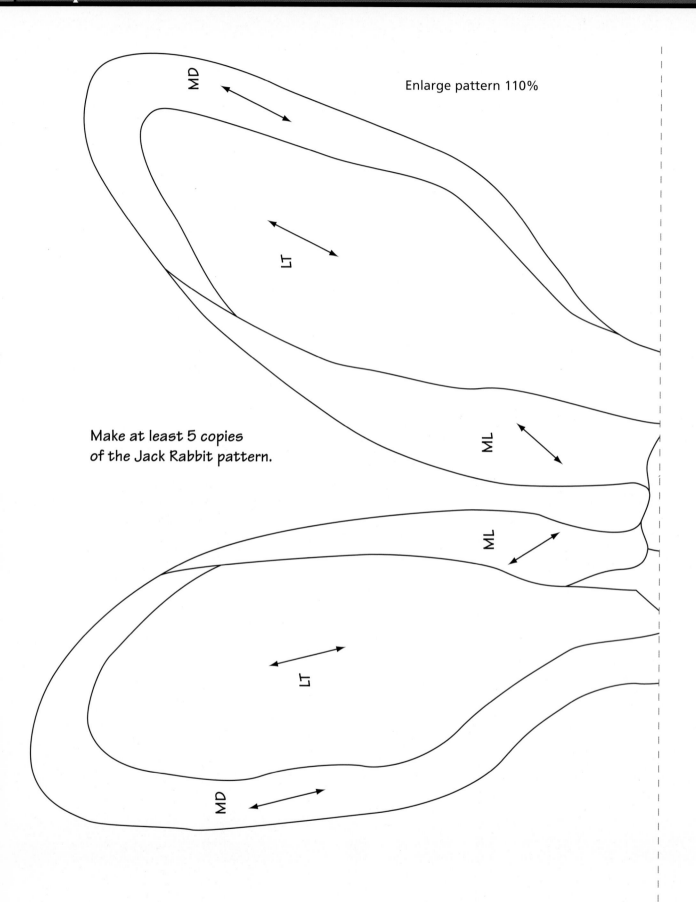

Enlarge pattern 110%

Make at least 5 copies
of the Jack Rabbit pattern.

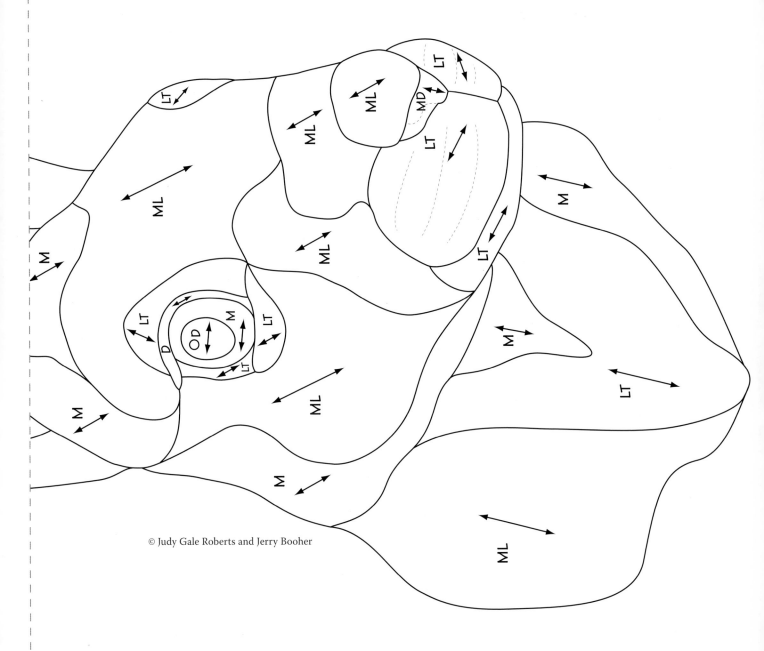

Legend	
←→	Grain direction
D	Dark shade of wood
MD	Medium dark shade of wood
M	Medium shade of wood
ML	Medium light shade of wood
LT	Light shade of wood

© Judy Gale Roberts and Jerry Booher

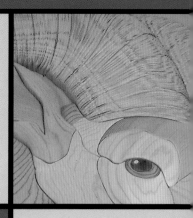

Big Horn Ram Project

Wood

- Dark shade of wood at least 2" wide by 2 ½" long and ¾" thick
- Medium-dark shade of wood at least 4" wide by 7" long and ¾" thick
- Medium shade of wood at least 8" wide by 9" long and ¾" thick
- Medium-light shade of wood at least 6" wide by 20" long and ¾" thick
- Light shade of wood at least 4" wide by 4" long and ¾" thick.
- White shade of wood at least 4" wide by 4" long and ¾" thick
- ¼" luan plywood for the backing and sanding shim

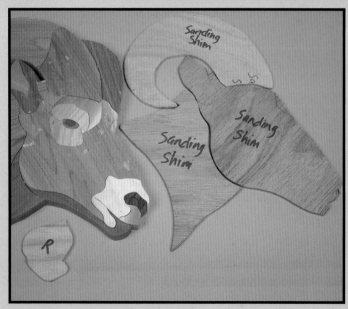

Photo 13.1. Sanding shims and raising shims are used on the Big Horn Ram. Use double-sided carpet tape to apply the parts to the sanding shims. Tape the eye parts to the raising shim. Blend the outer edges of the raised eye parts back down to the joining areas. The eye will be thicker. Sand the background horn first, then the neck, followed by the horn in the foreground. The head will be the last section sanded.

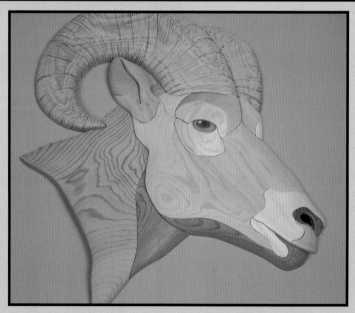

Photo 13.2. The Big Horn Ram has been finish sanded. The nostril was lowered, and texture was applied to the horns using the Wonder Wheel. The highlight was added to the eye, and the inside part of the ear was dished out to give a hollow look. The upper lip is slightly thicker than the lower lip.

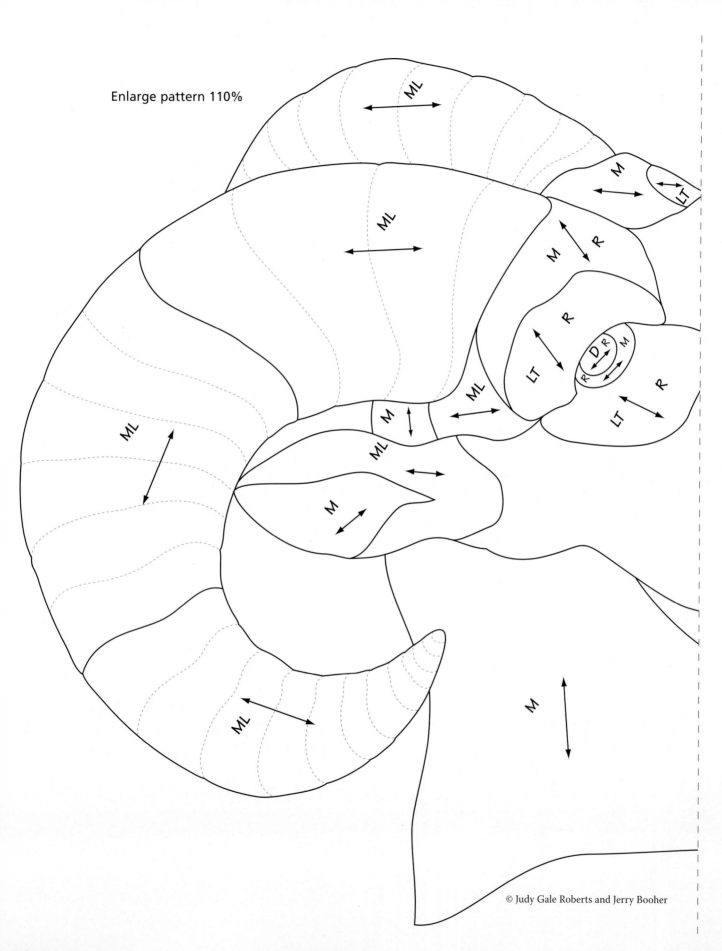

Enlarge pattern 110%

© Judy Gale Roberts and Jerry Booher

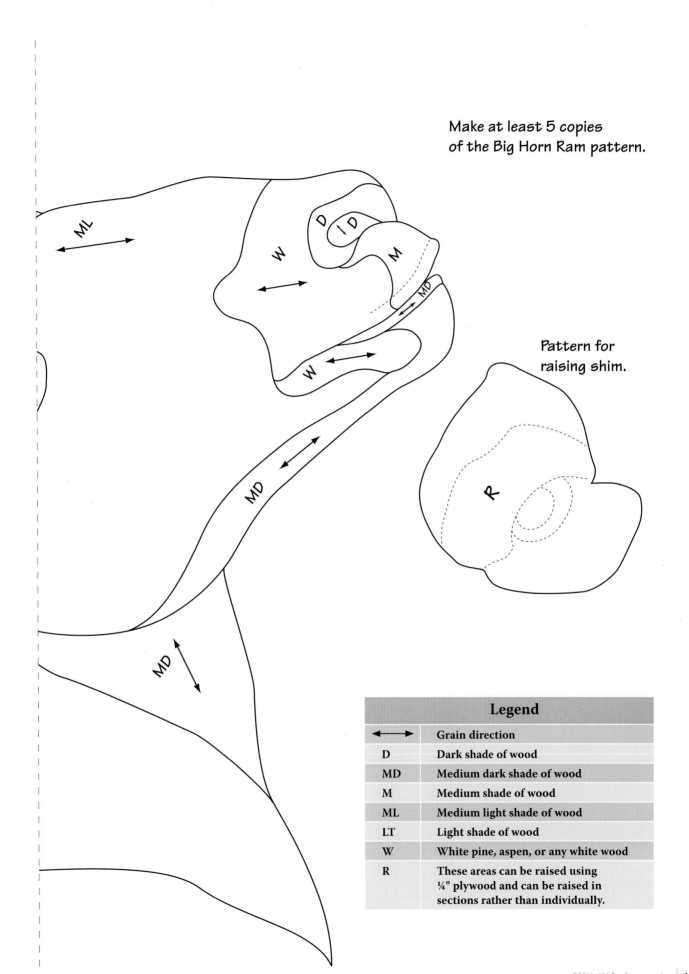

Make at least 5 copies
of the Big Horn Ram pattern.

Pattern for
raising shim.

Legend	
↔	Grain direction
D	Dark shade of wood
MD	Medium dark shade of wood
M	Medium shade of wood
ML	Medium light shade of wood
LT	Light shade of wood
W	White pine, aspen, or any white wood
R	These areas can be raised using ¼" plywood and can be raised in sections rather than individually.

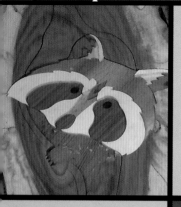

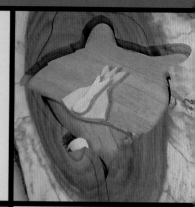

Raccoon Project

Wood

- Dark shade of wood at least 4 ½" wide by 9" long and ¾" thick
- Medium-dark shade of wood at least 6" wide by 5" long and ¾" thick
- Medium shade of wood at least 8" wide by 24" long and ¾" thick
- Light shade of wood at least 5" wide by 11" long and ¾" thick.
- White shade of wood at least 5" wide by 7" long and ¾" thick
- ¼" luan plywood for the backing and sanding shim
- Two ⅜"-diameter dowels cut approximately ¾" long (walnut dowel works best)

Photo 14.1. Raising shims are used on the Raccoon. Cut the raising shims smaller than the actual parts to be raised. The raising shims will work as the sanding shims. Use double-sided carpet tape to apply the parts to the shims.

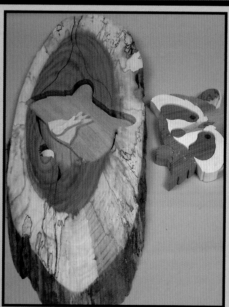

Photo 14.2. The raising shims are in place and are ready for the parts. If you have some log slices, or any piece of wood with natural edge, these will work great for the Raccoon.

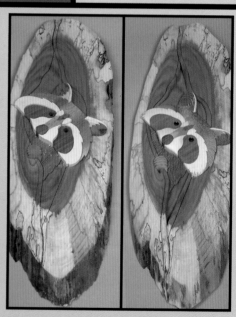

Photo 14.3. Use walnut dowels for the eyes. We added texture to the Raccoon. Coarser texture was applied to the coat and the outside edges of the face. If you want to add highlights to the eyes, it is easier to predrill the dowels before rounding them.

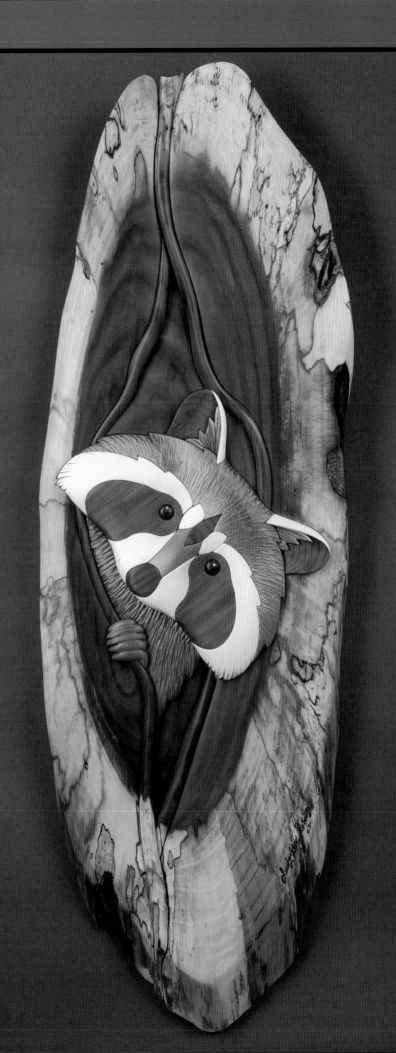

Make at least 5 copies
of the Raccoon pattern.

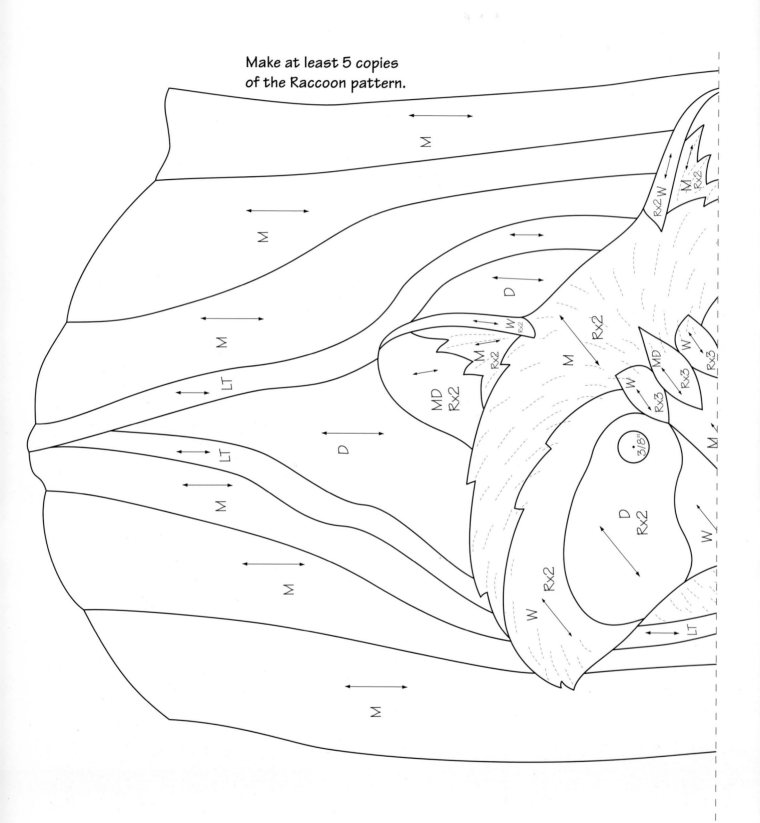

Enlarge pattern 110%

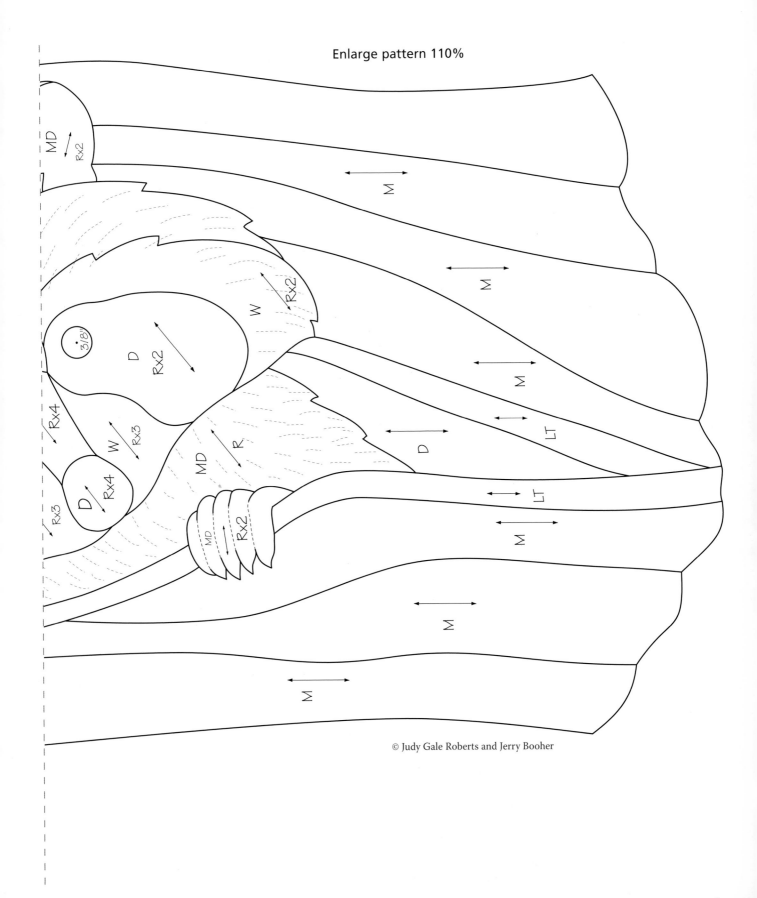

© Judy Gale Roberts and Jerry Booher

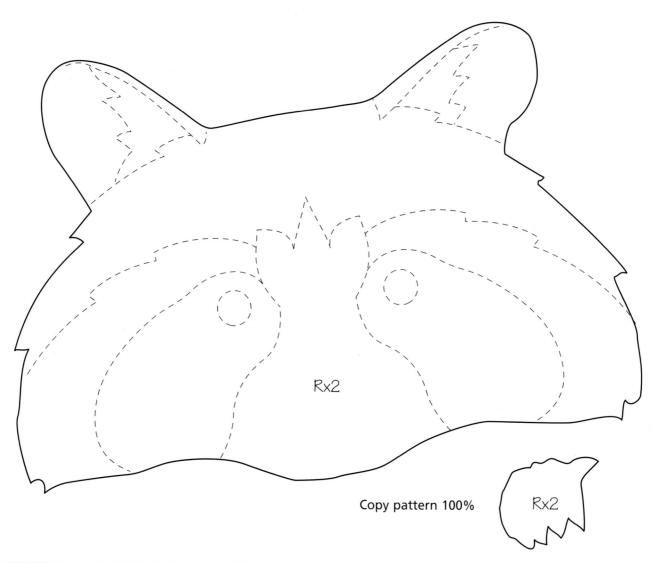

Rx2

Copy pattern 100%

Rx2

Legend	
⟷	Grain direction
D	Dark shade of wood
MD	Medium dark shade of wood
M	Medium shade of wood
LT	Light shade of wood
W	White pine, aspen, or any white wood
R	These areas can be raised using ¼" plywood and can be raised in sections rather than individually.
Rx2	Raise these areas an additional ¼" making a total of ½" in shims.
Rx3	Raise these areas an additional ¼" making a total of ¾" in shims.
Rx4	Raise these areas an additional ¼" making a total of 1" in shims.

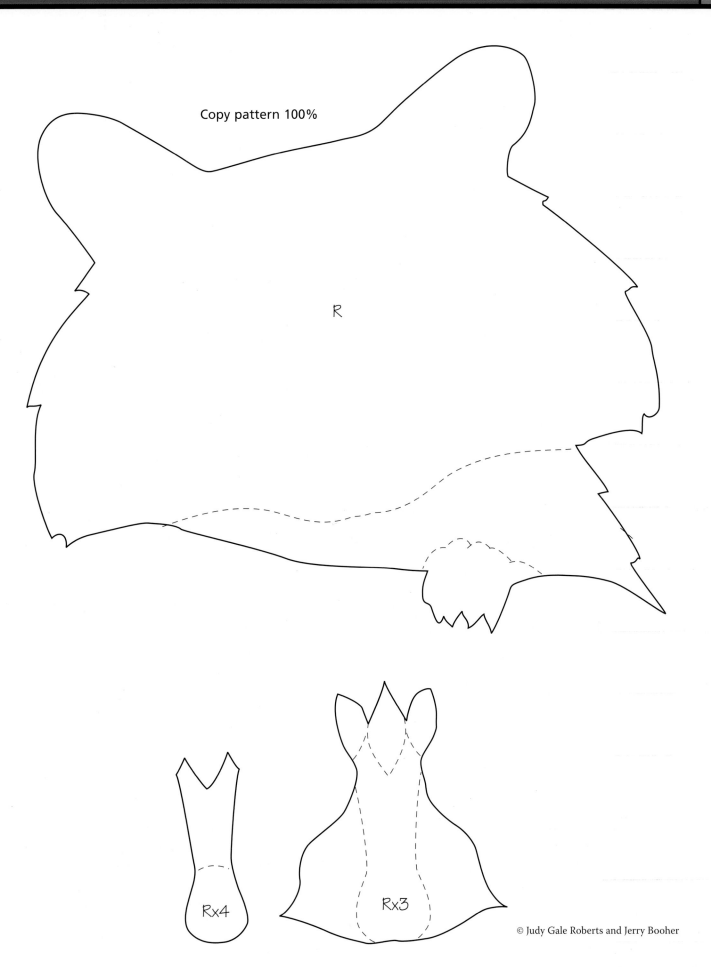

Copy pattern 100%

R

Rx4

Rx3

© Judy Gale Roberts and Jerry Booher

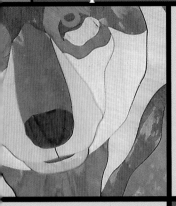

Wolf Project

Wood
- ■ Dark shade of wood at least 2 ½" wide by 4" long and ¾" thick
- ■ Medium-dark shade of wood at least 9" wide by 16" long and ¾" thick
- ■ Medium shade of wood at least 2 ½" wide by 5" long and ¾" thick
- ■ Light shade of wood at least 8" wide by 18" long and ¾" thick.
- ■ White shade of wood at least 8" wide by 8" long and ¾" thick
- ■ ¼" luan plywood for the backing and sanding shim

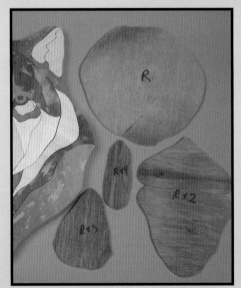

Photo 15.1. Raising shims are used on the Wolf. Cut the raising shims smaller than the actual parts to be raised. Tape the raising shims in place while sanding. The Wolf will look better if you blend the bridge of the nose back into the forehead. Use double-sided carpet tape to apply the parts, along with the raising shims, to the sanding shims (shown in the next photo).

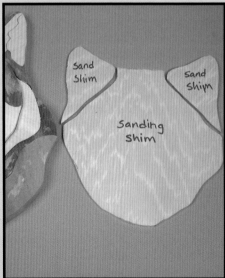

Photo 15.2. The raising shims are in place next to the sanding shims. Sand the neck area first before taping the face and the ears to the sanding shims.

Photo 15.3. The Wolf is finish sanded. Note the texture applied to the Wolf's coat. The pattern has dashed lines to follow as a guide. Also, the highlights are added to the eyes, the nostrils are lowered, and the transition from the forehead to the nose is smooth.

Make at least 6 copies of the Wolf pattern.

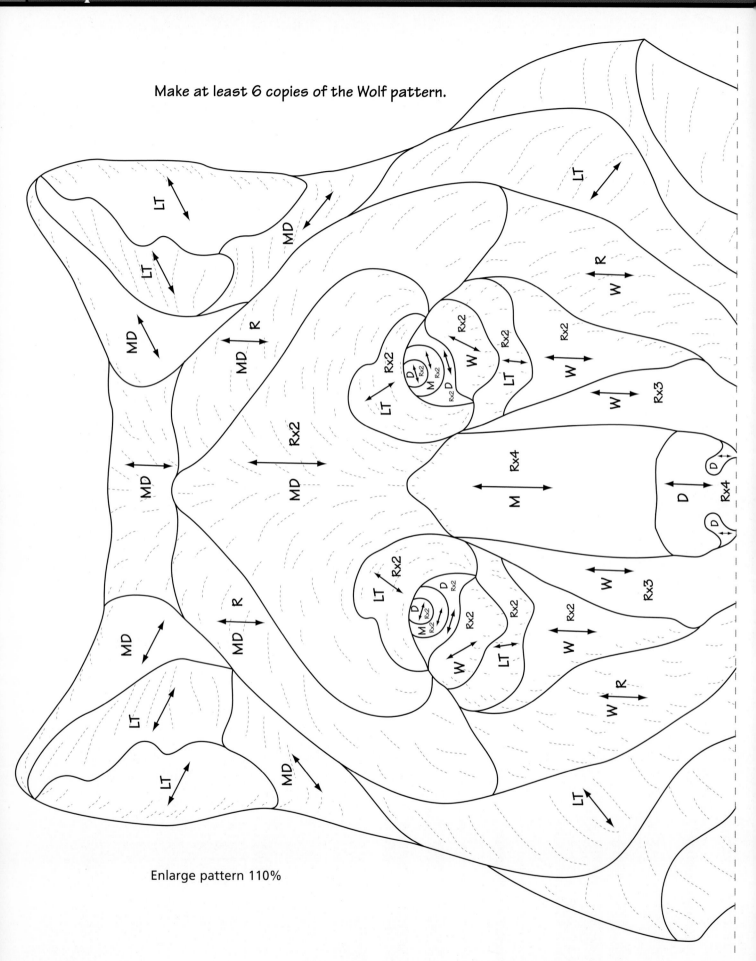

Enlarge pattern 110%

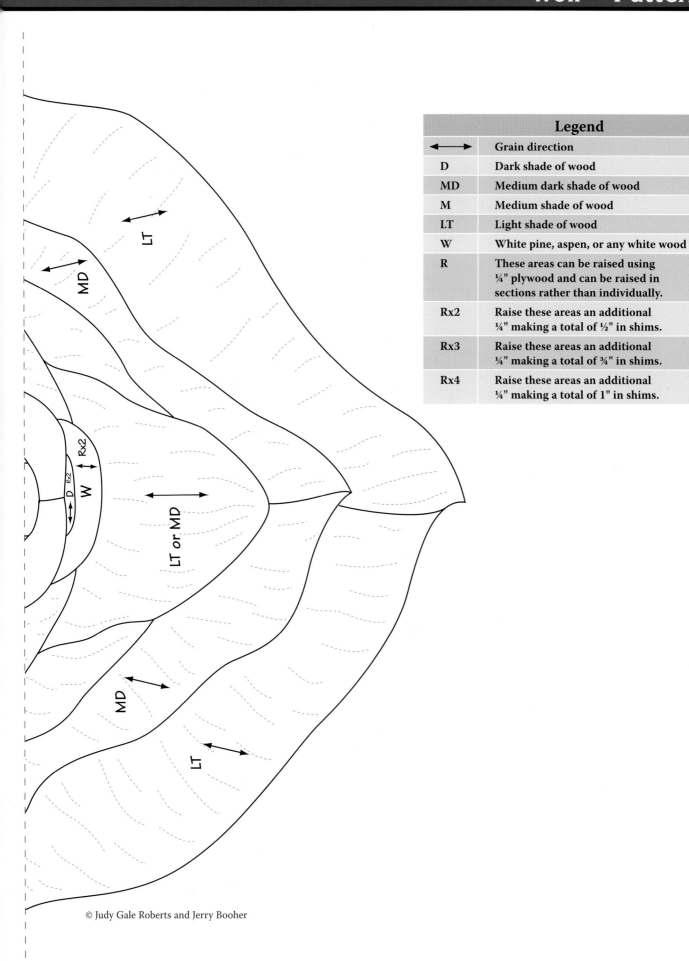

Legend	
↔	Grain direction
D	Dark shade of wood
MD	Medium dark shade of wood
M	Medium shade of wood
LT	Light shade of wood
W	White pine, aspen, or any white wood
R	These areas can be raised using ¼" plywood and can be raised in sections rather than individually.
Rx2	Raise these areas an additional ¼" making a total of ½" in shims.
Rx3	Raise these areas an additional ¼" making a total of ¾" in shims.
Rx4	Raise these areas an additional ¼" making a total of 1" in shims.

LT

MD

D

Rx2

W

Rx2

LT or MD

MD

LT

© Judy Gale Roberts and Jerry Booher

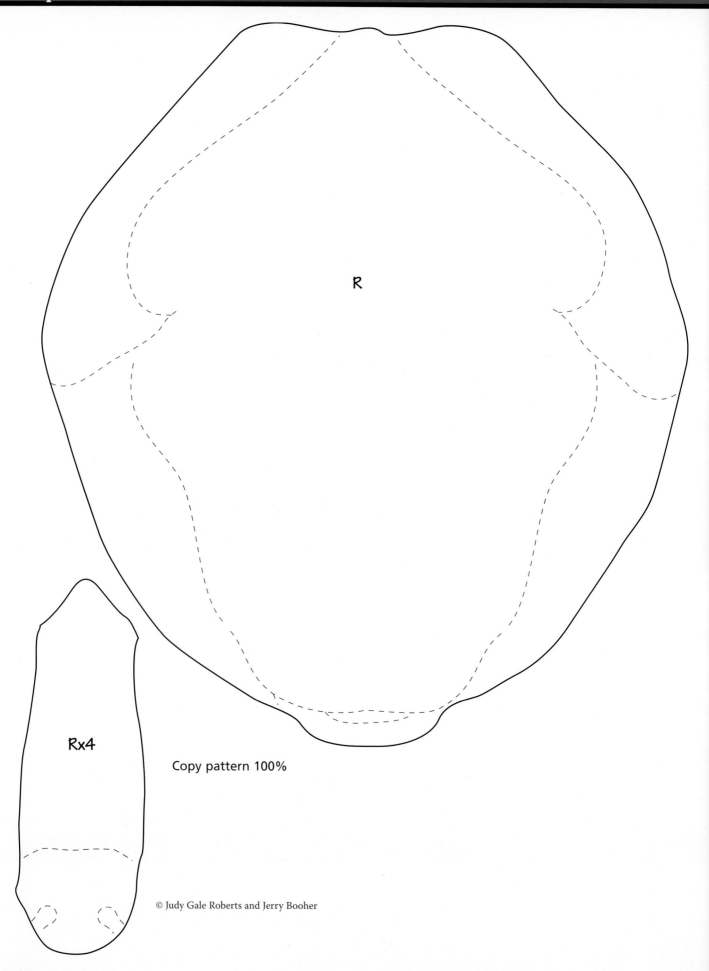

R

Rx4

Copy pattern 100%

© Judy Gale Roberts and Jerry Booher

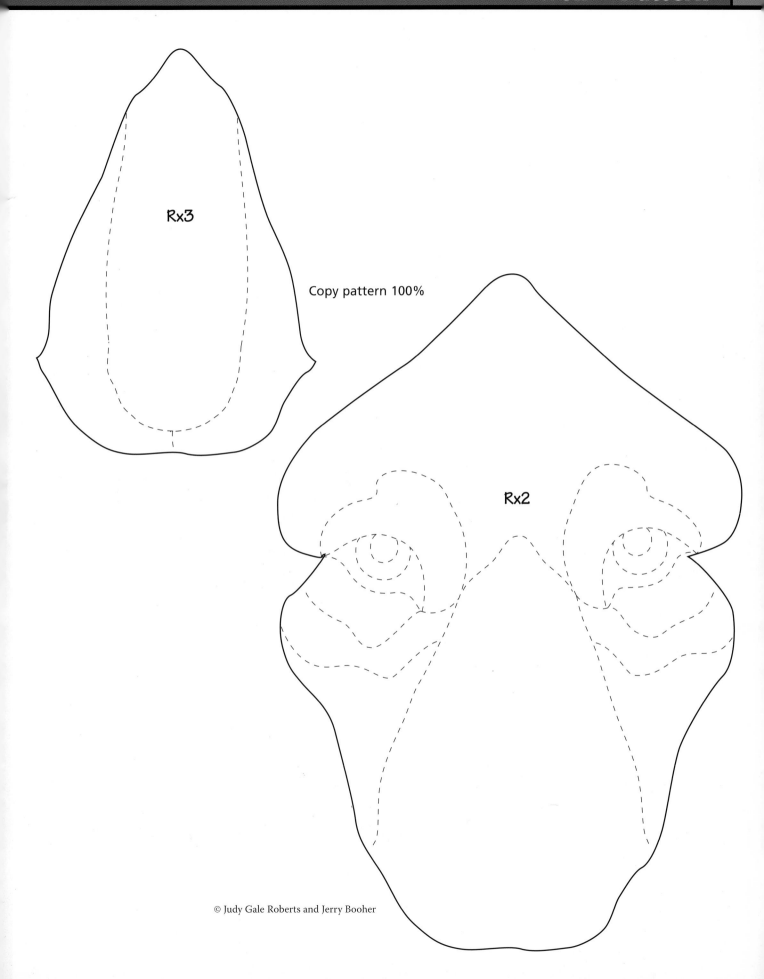

Rx3

Copy pattern 100%

Rx2

© Judy Gale Roberts and Jerry Booher

Resources

Be sure to visit Judy and Jerry's Website (**www.intarsia.com**) to see all of the projects in this book in 3-D, rotating format. This will be very helpful should you have a question about shaping any of these projects.

For a free copy of Judy and Jerry's Newsletter, *The Intarsia Times*, please call 800–316–9010, visit our Website at **www.intarsia.com**, or email **jerry@intarsia.com**.

Items available from Roberts Studio (800–316–9010):

Flex Drum Sander

On-Line Scroll Saw Blades

Old Masters Gel Finish

Wonder Wheel

Detail Sanders

Intarsia Patterns

400-Degree Hot Melt Glue Gun

Luxo Magnifier Light

On/Off Foot Switch

Excalibur Tilt Head 22" Scroll Saw

Other items used in this book:
Double-sided carpet tape, light duty plastic carpet tape – Ace Hardware, item #50106

6" Variable Speed Grinder, 2,000 rpm to 3,450 rpm – Delta, Model #23-655; Sears, Model #21152

Glue Stick – Scotch Re-stickable Adhesive, available at office supplies stores

Spray Adhesive – 3M Spray Mount Artist's adhesive, available at office supplies stores

Shoe Dye – Fiebing's, available at most shoe repair shops

1" Foam paint brushes – available at craft or painting stores/departments.